HUMAN HORIZONS SERIES

ALZHEIMER'S DISEASE

Coping with a Living Death

ROBERT T. WOODS

A CONDOR BOOK
SOUVENIR PRESS (E & A) LTD

NOTE: Throughout this book dementia sufferers, their carers and doctors have been referred to interchangeably as 'he' or 'she', to emphasise that they may be of either sex.

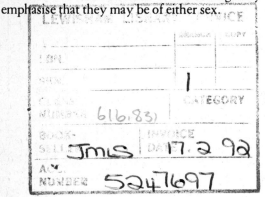

Contents

Alzheimer's Disease: a fact sheet

— Alzheimer's Disease (AD) is the most common form of a group of conditions, all affecting the brain, known as the dementias.

— AD is also known as: Senile Dementia Alzheimer's Type (SDAT); in younger people the 'Senile' is omitted.

— About one in five of the over 75s suffer from some form of dementia.

— Many well known figures in public life have suffered from AD at the end of their lives.

— There is no known cure for AD.

— Most AD sufferers are cared for at home, often by other family members.

— AD can affect people in their 30s, 40s or 50s, though it becomes more common with increasing age.

— Problems with memory and learning are often the most noticeable symptoms, but there may also be changes in personality, a loss of practical skills, problems in communication and loss of 'common sense'.

— AD is a disorder involving progressive decline; AD sufferers are likely to become more and more disabled as time goes on.

— There has been a huge growth of research on AD over the last ten years; hopes of a breakthrough are growing.

— Carers have found great support in recent years from other carers through self-help groups like the Alzheimer's Disease Society.

— Support services are being developed, although not quickly enough to cope with the growth of the problem.

Introduction

Alzheimer's Disease: a progressive reduction in the ability to think, remember, learn and reason, leading to a reduced capacity for self-care and self-direction.

Alzheimer's Disease (AD) is a tragic condition. In the UK it is estimated that 750,000 people suffer from this devastating disease and its related conditions. The tragedy of AD arises from a number of sources:

1 The disability can be extremely severe.
2 A very large number of people are afflicted already, and AD threatens to hit countless others in the future.
3 Not only the sufferer, but also those who care for them, their family and loved ones, have their entire world turned upside down by it. The tragedy is doubled as they see the person's abilities disintegrate and as they endeavour to provide the increasing levels of care the person will require.
4. Among the general public there has been an almost complete ignorance of AD and its consequences.
5 This ignorance has been matched by a neglect of AD by most health-service and social-service professionals.
6 There has been insufficient allocation of resources to meet current needs, or the greater needs predicted for the future.
7 Basic research into the condition and its causes has only recently begun to be seriously developed.

One wife of a man with AD said: 'It's as if John is dead in a way — he's certainly no longer the man I married. But his body is still here. It's like a living death.'

Many carers express similar sentiments. When so many

abilities, skills and capacities are lost, it becomes difficult to perceive the person with whom the carer has enjoyed a relationship for so long as the same human being. When a loved one dies, of course, there is a funeral: friends and family share their grief. Over a period of time, the painful adjustment to the loss takes place. When Alzheimer's Disease strikes a family, its members are faced with a fairly long period of time in which, far from adjusting to the loss of the loved one, they may well be desperately trying to cope with a progressive decline in the person's remaining abilities. There is often little recognition from society in general, and even from friends and family, of the difficulties being experienced.

This book aims to help those who are faced with this unenviable experience. It provides basic information about Alzheimer's Disease and related disorders on the assumption that coping is easier when you are well informed. In addition, there are chapters that suggest possible ways of managing some of the problems encountered in caring for the person with AD, and on dealing with some of the feelings—the stresses and emotional strain, for example—that may accompany having an AD sufferer in the family. Although written primarily for those who are involved in caring day-to-day for an AD sufferer, the book will also be relevant to those not so directly involved, and to those who simply wish to have a greater appreciation of what the carer is experiencing. Thus relatives living at a distance, or for one reason or another not providing care, friends, and those helping in a paid or a voluntary capacity may also find something of interest here.

Nothing can ever be said or done to make AD a painless experience—for sufferer or carer. There are, however, a number of ways in which the pain may be relieved a little, stress and anxiety reduced, and ways of finding more appropriate help. There is no cure for AD and no easy solutions to the many problems it poses. Every case is unique. AD cannot be adequately diagnosed within the compass of a book such as this—there can be no substitute for skilled, thorough medical investigation. The book can, however, offer the assurance that AD and its related conditions are beginning to be taken seriously at last; that it is now increasingly recognised as a disorder to be tackled; and that research into its basic causes, potential methods of treatment, and the best ways of providing the care required, is under way in a number of centres throughout the world. Carers often feel they are alone in their plight. It may be of some encouragement to know that there are thousands of carers in a similar position.

At this point the author must make an admission. I have never cared for an AD sufferer 24 hours a day. I have never had my sleep disturbed night after night, or faced days of repeated questioning. This is not therefore a book about one carer's experiences of facing this awesome disease. If it has any value, it will be because over the last 14 years I have spoken to many people—in carers' groups and individually—who have experienced these and all the other difficulties AD brings. I have tried to listen to their concerns, their burdens, their moments of success. I am grateful to them for all they have taught me, and I hope this book communicates something of their emotions, their resourcefulness and their courage.

The book aims to help people think through what they are doing and come to a realistic appraisal of what they can and cannot offer the AD sufferer: what can be achieved and what is likely to be irretrievable. It could be used to help a family work together as a team in supporting the sufferer. It could also help those outside the family to understand what those carrying out the caring role are experiencing.

It is often useful to be able to discuss what you read about a condition such as AD with an experienced person who knows the sufferer well. Such a person can help you relate what you read—which is, necessarily, in general terms—to your own situation. A book such as this cannot answer all your questions, but it can help you to be sufficiently well informed to know what questions you need to be asking of the professionals involved in your case.

An issue that often arises when giving information about AD is how optimistic a picture should be painted of the future. At an early stage—perhaps when the diagnosis has just been tentatively made—is it better for the family to know how awful it could be, how much the sufferer could deteriorate? Or is it better to emphasise the varied rates of deterioration, the possible periods of stability? Does the blackest and least hopeful scenario help the relative, allowing them to prepare for the worst? Or, alternatively, does it overwhelm the relative, and in fact prevent them coping with the changes and the difficulties? This book will take the middle road, encouraging the reader to prepare for the worst—but expect and hope for the best! It is hard to conceive of AD as a bed of roses, but over the centuries men and women have shown the most amazing capacity to find positive virtues in the midst of adversity, and we too will try to identify some of the satisfactions—the small successes and even those moments of joy—that can be experienced along this difficult road.

Alzheimer's Disease — a growth area

The best news for carers and sufferers (short of a cure) is that attention is at last beginning to be focused on AD. Perhaps most significantly, it is now realised that the number of sufferers is actually growing.

AD—like many other diseases—is more common in older people, particularly those over the age of 75. In many developed countries, there has already been a major increase in the number of people over retirement age (60 or 65). In the UK, the proportion of the population over 65 is now fairly stable, but an even more significant change is now occurring. The number of people aged 75 and over is growing rapidly. This means that the average old person is now rather older than in previous years!

Population projections in the UK (based on the 1981 census) show a small increase in the total number of people of pensionable age (3.3 per cent) between 1981 and 2001, a much bigger increase in the over 75s (27.6 per cent), and a massive increase of 79 per cent in the over 85s. When one also considers the fact that AD and its related conditions are at least five times more likely in a person over 80, compared with someone in their 60s, the reason for the increasing numbers of sufferers becomes evident (figs. 1 and 2). In the next few decades, other countries will also be affected dramatically as their proportion of old and very old people rises. The number of cases in Australia, for example, is expected to double between 1981 and 2001. And in years to come, countries not yet experiencing the disorder to any great extent—China, for

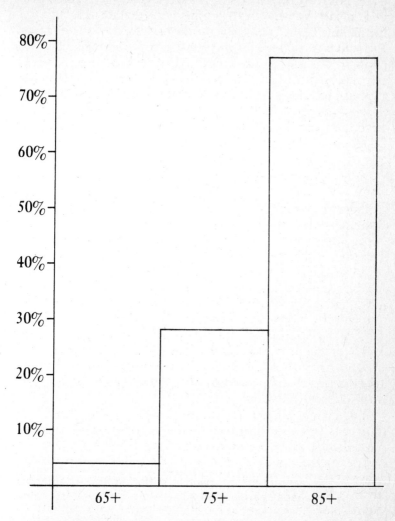

Fig. 1 Between the years 1981 and 2001, there will be only a small percentage increase in Britain in the total numbers of people over 65, but much larger percentage increases in the total numbers over 75, and especially over 85

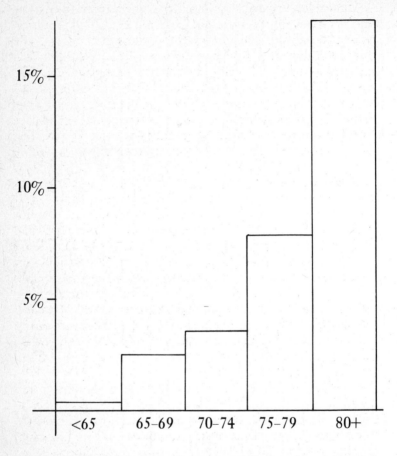

Fig. 2 The percentage of people suffering from dementia increases sharply with age

example, which has the fastest projected growth rate of older people in the world—will face the problem too.

Alongside the increasing numbers come increasing costs — community support services, hospital and residential provision are an expensive part of health and social services budgets. The cost in human terms is of course massive, but it is the financial cost which may eventually persuade those in power to take action. Thus in Canada with around 300,000 sufferers it is estimated that the cost runs up to 1.5 billion dollars each year. In the USA, with around 1.5 million sufferers, the expenditure is of the unimaginable order of 50 billion dollars! The amount spent on research has been, in comparative terms, minute.

An important obstacle to AD becoming widely known was its association with senility, the notion that loss of memory and confusion are in some way a normal expectation in old age. It is true that AD is more common in old age, but this does not make it a part of it, any more than other conditions like arthritis, diabetes or Parkinson's Disease would be considered part of the normal ageing process. As we shall discuss at length in Chapter 1, AD is not the end result of the ageing process, but a disease which can strike long before old age begins. The notion of senility led to inaction, no expectation of treatment, feelings of hopelessness and fear. AD, on the other hand, can be diagnosed, understood, distinguished from other similar but already treatable conditions, researched and—in time—alleviated with specific treatments.

A further obstacle is that AD has never been thought of as a 'killer disease'. In the UK, for example, it would seldom be seen on a death certificate as a cause of death. Most sufferers are said to die from some other condition—often bronchial pneumonia—but there is little doubt that, especially in younger people, the person's life will have been shortened by AD. In Canada, AD is now viewed as the fourth major cause of death—after heart disease, cancer and strokes. It is seen as leading, at least indirectly, to death in 10,000–20,000 Canadians a year. Certainly from this angle it is a life-threatening disease; in any terms, it is a disease that destroys the life of the sufferer and devastates the family involved. Viewed in this way, it may take its place amongst the major threats to health and life.

One of the most important positive factors has been the growing transformation of the carers in our society from a quiescent, impotent, submissive group of isolated individuals to an increasingly powerful pressure group, with strong political lobbying, championing the rights of carers to decent levels of support in making the currently popular 'community care' policies viable. This emergence of carers as a pressure group has brought to light conditions that were previously 'kept in the family', and drawn the attention of a wider audience. Thus in the UK, the Alzheimer's Disease Society was only formed in 1979, and has grown and developed tremendously in a very small space of time. Similarly, the Alzheimer Society of Canada was founded only in 1978. In 10 years these societies and others like them in the USA and Australia have made great progress, and their impact has begun to be felt.

In 1984, AD was the subject of a debate in the House of Commons, where the role of the Alzheimer's Disease Society was highly praised. For once, there was agreement on all sides. In the words of one government minister: AD 'can, should and must eventually be reversible. We must work, through research, to prevent its ravages; and we must in the meantime do all that we can to provide the best care to those who are suffering its ravages now.' Another speaker emphasised the need to increase public awareness.

In the USA there has been much greater government action (a dementia month, a Presidential task force, etc.) and much coverage in the media. This has been helped by celebrities admitting publicly their own association with the disease. The most notable example has been the revelation that celebrated film star Rita Hayworth suffered from AD. Her daughter, Princess Yasmin Aga Khan has played a prominent part in promoting the cause of the Alzheimer Disease and Related Disorders Society in the USA, and internationally through Alzheimer's Disease International, the federation of Alzheimer Societies world-wide. In 1986, at an Alzheimer's Society meeting in London, the actor Jack Lemmon revealed that his wife's mother was a sufferer, resulting in further publicity about the condition.

Interestingly, there have been fewer revelations of this kind in the UK. It has been suggested that Winston Churchill suffered from dementia for some years prior to his death, but the facts remain shrouded in mystery. There is no doubt that celebrities can help draw the public's attention to AD. Changing public awareness and attitudes is a long, slow task, which good media coverage can help.

It is not only the public who need to be made aware of the problem—the professionals have been slow to take a real interest in AD. In medical circles, the disease does not fall neatly into one speciality. Generally speaking, doctors have been less interested in problems affecting older people, and in conditions that take a long down-hill course. AD has suffered neglect on both counts. Worse still, people with such conditions were (and, regrettably, still are) sometimes regarded as potential 'bed-blockers', occupying an acute hospital bed required for more urgent cases. There was pressure then not to admit such cases in the first place. People with AD were likely to be rejected by the hospital services rather than be offered proper medical attention. The problem was seen simply as one of containing these patients, not to seek to develop expertise in this sort of condition.

Generation after generation of medical students were brought up in virtual ignorance of AD, whilst having detailed knowledge of many other much rarer diseases. In recent years, however, a number of psychiatrists, geriatricians and neurologists in the UK have developed a special interest in the diagnosis, care and management of these disorders, and are beginning to create a more positive climate in the medical world—where attitudes often take a very long time to change! (Similar changes are occurring in nursing, social work, occupational therapy, physiotherapy, speech therapy and clinical psychology.) There is a long, long way to go before it is seen as a highly desirable field in which to work. Training courses are beginning to include more about AD, but this is not saying much, as there was so little beforehand!

There is then a gradually increasing awareness of a growing problem, and recognition of the need for not just more but better services. Research efforts must be multiplied when there is a condition about which so little is known, but which is so cruel in its effects. A report from the UK's Health Advisory

Service on the problem was graphically entitled 'The Rising Tide'. There are hopeful signs that action, political and professional, is beginning to take place—at last.

What's in a name?

In the UK, the reaction to the name 'Alzheimer's Disease' is usually one of puzzlement—even among some members of the caring professions, let alone the general public. Why not simply call it 'senile dementia', as it's always been called? some say. Others object strongly to the word 'dementia', pointing out that the dictionary definition of demented (driven mad, crazy, insane) is not at all apt for the sufferer. Others argue that there are (as we shall see in Chapter 1) a number of conditions leading to rather similar problems. This has led to the adoption of the name 'Alzheimer's Disease and Related Disorders' by several carers' organisations. Some doctors have used quite different terminology: chronic brain failure, chronic brain syndrome, organic brain syndrome, chronic confusion, senile psychosis and so on have all enjoyed some popularity. Service planners tend to refer to the Elderly Severely Mentally Infirm (shortened at times to ESMI) or just Elderly Mentally Infirm (EMI).

Does it matter what these conditions are called? Certainly there has to be sufficient agreement for it to be possible to communicate with carers, professionals and the public in order to increase awareness and understanding. I have found the use of 'Alzheimer's Disease' (with the occasional reference to related disorders!) very helpful indeed for a number of reasons:

1 It encourages people to look afresh at what is of course an old problem, and to re-think their own ideas about the condition.
2 By making the link with a condition known to affect younger people, it does not limit the discussion to old age or ageing processes.
3 It is possible for the public to learn a difficult name for an important group of disorders if it is aired sufficiently.
4 Alzheimer Societies are becoming established in many countries.

5 The idea of a specific, named disease is useful—it encourages people to look at the possibilities of research and treatment.

6 Relatives often seem to find it more helpful to blame a disease for the person's difficulties, rather than blaming it on a stage of a person's life.

In this book the abbreviation AD is used for the sake of simplicity. Carers should be aware that professionals may continue to use different terminology. In particular they will, understandably, continue to use dementia as the family name for all these disorders, feeling perhaps that AD is more specific than they are able to be. With less justification, and little practical utility, some will doubtless continue to use 'pre-senile' and 'senile' as ways of describing dementia. These words are used to indicate whether the condition developed before or after some arbitrarily chosen age limit (usually 65).

Some carers become concerned that AD sufferers are often given medical care by psychiatrists. After all, they protest, it is not a mental illness. In a strict sense it does of course affect the person's mind; in fact, strictly speaking, the literal translation of dementia as 'out of one's mind' isn't really inaccurate. The complication is that unlike many (but not all) psychiatric conditions, we have some knowledge of its actual impact on the brain. There seems little point in arguing whether it is a mental illness or a neurological disease. The priority must be to make sure that sufferers receive the best possible care and treatment. To achieve this there will undoubtedly need to be collaboration between professionals of many specialities, working with a variety of facilities. How AD is described is secondary to obtaining the very best for both sufferers and their supporters.

Chapter One

Alzheimer's Disease and other dementias

AD is the most common of a family of conditions known collectively as the 'dementias'. This chapter aims to describe the main features of these disorders and what is known about their causes. Sometimes people think that because there is as yet no treatment for AD, it is pointless to seek medical advice and help. In fact, a full medical assessment in all cases is so important that it can never be considered an optional extra. The reasons for this are set out in full.

Every type of dementia has one thing in common: a loss of intellectual power. Typically, this leads to a variety of problems, including difficulties in remembering, making decisions, thinking through complex ideas, carrying out practical tasks, and retaining new information or acquiring new skills. This loss is usually progressive, with further decline becoming obvious as time goes on.

In about half of the elderly people who suffer from dementia, AD can be identified as the primary cause. In a fifth, Multi-Infarct Dementia (MID) is the major condition. In a further fifth, changes due to both AD and MID are found in the person's brain (see Fig. 3). There is little evidence of differences between countries in the rates of dementia that cannot be accounted for by the much smaller proportion of older people in developing countries. However, in Japan, whilst the rate of dementia is roughly the same as in Western countries, there are reports that, unlike in the West, MID is more common than AD. The nature of MID, and some of the rarer conditions that make up the other tenth of cases of dementia, will be described before discussing AD in detail.

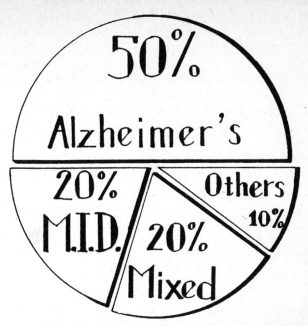

Fig. 3 Alzheimer's Disease is the most common form of dementia; it occurs alone or together with Multi-Infarct Dementia in around 70 per cent of elderly people with dementia

Multi-infarct dementia

An infarct occurs when an area of tissue—in this instance brain tissue—has been destroyed. Each infarct results from a stroke, where the blood supply is cut off to that particular area of the brain. Without its vital blood supply the cells are permanently damaged. Multi-infarct dementia results from a series of small 'strokelets' creating a number of areas of dead cells in the brain. The strokes may well arise from 'hardening of the arteries', the gradual clogging of the arterial blood vessels. If a piece of debris (an embolus) breaks off and is carried with the circulating blood supply to the brain, it may block one of the smaller blood vessels supplying the brain. The other cause of a stroke is when a blood vessel in the brain becomes weak and bursts. The blood, released from its proper channels, flows into areas where, far from bringing life, it actually destroys brain tissue.

Each stroke or strokelet may in itself be quite minor, but the accumulation of damage results in symptoms of dementia. As well as actually destroying some cells, others are temporarily impaired by the partial loss of blood. In time, the recovery of these cells may allow some recovery of function between episodes. This may lead to an apparently step-wise deterioration, rather than the smoother decline associated with AD. Some patients will have episodes where a further stroke nearly happens, but the blood supply returns before permanent damage occurs. This is called a Transient Ischaemic Attack (TIA). The person's speech or movement on one side of the body may be temporarily affected, but after a short time he returns to his former state.

The disabilities the person has suffered will be influenced by which parts of the brain are damaged by the strokes. It has been suggested that about 5 per cent of the brain tissue can be damaged without apparently preventing normal function—as long as certain key areas are spared. If a tenth of the brain is damaged, MID is almost certain to occur. Most of the more familiar memory, learning, speech and language problems arise from damage to the cortex, the outermost layer of the brain. The cortex is supplied with blood by some of the larger blood vessels. When some of the smaller blood vessels are involved, parts of the brain beneath the cortex (the sub-cortical areas) may be damaged. This gives rise to less obvious, but important, difficulties in carrying out tasks, a general slowness and lethargy, together with some forgetfulness. The different effects of blockage of the small and large vessels, and the effects of different areas being damaged in each patient, means that each person with MID will have a slightly different pattern of disabilities. Their problems are likely to be less general and widespread than in AD; they are more likely to have some abilities that are noticeably preserved; they are more likely to be frustrated by their difficulties, and to have outbursts of intense emotion—floods of tears for instance.

Causes:
A series of small strokes, destroying brain tissue, arising from disorders of the heart and blood circulation system.

Risk factors:
1 High blood pressure (hypertension) is a major risk factor for all types of stroke.
2 Other problems in blood circulation or heart disease.
3 More common in men.
4 Diabetes increase the risk.
5 Heart disease risk factors (i.e., smoking, being overweight, too little exercise, unhealthy diet, etc).
6 Family history—close relatives having heart disease increases the risk of heart disease, and so the risk of MID.

Prevention:
A healthy life-style! If blood pressure tends to be high, it is important to take steps to reduce this, either by medication or—preferably—by adopting a more relaxed, less stressful lifestyle.

Diagnosis:
A history of previous strokes, high blood pressure and a sudden beginning to the problem are amongst the features of a dementia that would make it more likely to be MID than AD. There are also certain neurological features, including disturbances of vision, slurred speech and weakness of limbs, which are more common in MID. Sometimes the infarcts are large enough to be seen on a CT scan (see p. 36), but because the scan is not sensitive enough to pick up smaller infarcts, MID may still be present even if the scan shows no infarcts.

Treatment:
The emphasis in the treatment of MID is to prevent further strokes. Medication to reduce the blood pressure from a high level could be helpful, as would appropriate treatment of any heart condition. Certain medications help prevent blood forming the clots that lead to the blockages described previously—among them is the familiar aspirin, for once not being used to reduce pain. If diabetes is present, steps should be taken by diet/medication to reduce the level of blood sugar.

Other Dementias

PICK'S DISEASE

Named after Arnold Pick, who described the condition at the beginning of this century. Examination of the person's brain is necessary to confirm its presence. Under the microscope, some of the neurons are seen to be unusually enlarged, with various parts of the normal cell mixed up in a disorganised fashion. These abnormal cells are called Pick bodies, and are a distinctive feature of the disease. In addition, various parts of the brain often have a shrunken appearance—particularly at the front. In common with AD, the disease effectively puts out of action a large number of brain cells.

As with all the dementias, there is usually a progressive loss of abilities. In Pick's Disease, memory problems seem to develop at a later stage. Early on, there may be a loss of judgement, leading to the person appearing rather silly, or putting themselves in dangerous situations without any concern for safety. The person may behave in socially inappropriate ways, losing his judgement or becoming unconcerned about what is and is not acceptable in different situations. He may seem not to care about anything. Behaviour may become quite repetitive and at times bizarre. Appetites may be greatly increased. Later, problems of speech emerge; carrying out practical tasks becomes more difficult. The disease is most common in the 50–60 age group. It is quite rare in older people. The person's life-expectancy is reduced, with the disease lasting on average about seven years from onset to death. As with any average, longer (and shorter) durations do occur.

At present, little is known regarding causes, risk factors or treatment. In some cases, it can be diagnosed correctly whilst the person is alive from the appearance of the brain on a brain scan, together with the presence of these distinctive features of behaviour mentioned above.

BINSWANGER'S DISEASE

This condition was first described at the end of the last century, but it is now being recognised more frequently. Its effects can often be seen on a CT scan. It is similar to MID, and the patient is likely to have suffered from raised blood pressure. The blood vessels blocked and damaged are those supplying the innermost regions of the brain (the white matter, as opposed to the grey matter in the outer layers). The person is often quite disabled, but more through lethargy and apathy than lack of ability. She may at times appear quite manic, swinging from apathy to periods of over-activity, loss of inhibitions and jollity. There is less in the way of memory impairment, and the progression may be quite slow, with lengthy periods of stability between strokes.

CREUTZFELDT-JAKOB DISEASE

This is a very rare condition (affecting less than one person in a million) that occurs most often before the age of 60. It is worth mentioning mainly because it has been shown that it can be transferred from one person to another. Its cause is thought to be a form of virus; however, there is virtually no danger of the virus being passed from person to person by every-day contact.

The condition results in the brain developing a sponge-like appearance on examination under the microscope, with neurons and other brain cells being destroyed. Some cases progress extremely quickly, death occurring within 18 months. Other cases may be slower, up to 15 years being reported. The loss of memory, verbal and practical abilities and loss of recognition are very severe; epileptic fits and muscle spasms are common. Finally, the patient becomes very disabled, hardly able to move, and almost completely unaware of her environment. There is no treatment at present. In some patients there is a family history of the condition. These cases tend to progress more slowly than where it is the first occurrence in a family.

NEUROSYPHILIS

At the turn of the century, General Paralysis of the Insane (GPI) was among the commonest conditions to be found in any large mental hospital. Patients had memory lapses, speech problems and a variety of other symptoms. Today it is a rare condition, although cases do still occur. It was common in soldiers and officers returning from the Napoleonic Wars, but did not turn out to be due to the terrors of war or even drinking to excess! In 1913, the bacterium that causes the sexually transmitted disease syphilis was identified in the brains of GPI sufferers. The disease was finally proved to be the final stage of untreated syphilis, perhaps 20 or 40 years after the initial infection. With the advent of penicillin, most cases of syphilis did not progress to GPI. Even when this does occur, the bacteria can still be destroyed by penicillin injections, with some improvement likely, depending on the degree of permanent damage to brain structures. There are simple blood-tests available to screen for this condition, which are used almost routinely because effective treatment is available for this form of dementia.

ALCOHOL-RELATED DEMENTIAS

Excessive drinking over a period of years can lead to a range of problems affecting memory, learning and other abilities. Some of the difficulties are thought to arise from the nutritional problems which accompany chronic alcohol abuse. For example, in Korsakoff's psychosis key parts of the brain's memory system suffer damage due to deficiencies in certain vitamins. The person is left with little ability to learn new things, although their other abilities may be relatively intact. Other problems may arise from the person's damaged liver, allowing chemicals toxic to the brain to circulate. Heavy drinkers are more likely to suffer head injuries, damaging further an already vulnerable brain. The brains of alcoholics are often shrunken, particularly at the front, and there can be a change in personality as well as intellect. The problems can be reversible to some extent; complete abstinence from alcohol and replacement of the vitamins and other nutrients can lead to at least a partial recovery.

HUNTINGTON'S DISEASE

The major feature of this disorder is abnormal movements. The person's limbs move and jerk about in an uncontrolled fashion, causing more disability than the dementia itself, which arises at a later stage. The person has great difficulty feeding or dressing, and may become very frustrated with his inability to make simple movements. There is a shrinkage of particular brain areas associated with this distressing condition.

Most cases develop when the person is between 35 and 45, which leads to one of the saddest aspects of the disease. It is a condition with a very high genetic factor. In fact, each sufferer's child has a 50 per cent chance of developing the disease also. Unfortunately, at the usual child-rearing age, the potential parent does not know whether or not he or she will contract the disease later and so whether or not their own children will be at risk.

Diagnostic tests are being developed in an attempt to identify sufferers before the symptoms become apparent. This raises a number of problems for potential sufferers and their families; and counselling regarding the risks for each family member is very important. Any readers who have a relative with Huntingdon's Disease should contact the relevant association (Combat in the UK) for information and advice (see Appendix).

PARKINSON'S DISEASE

Parkinson's Disease (PD) is primarily a disorder of movement, caused by damage to a part of the brain that has a vital role in the control of movement. Its features often include uncontrollable shakiness in the hands, difficulty in starting an action, slow walking, rigidity, and indistinct speech. The identification of a chemical deficiency offered the possibility of treatment for PD by the use of a replacement substance called L-dopa. This has turned out not to be a cure, although it may reduce the difficulties for some time.

Originally PD sufferers, whilst certainly disabled, were thought not to be dementing. Their intellect, memory and so on were regarded as intact. Now there are strong indications that a proportion of PD sufferers do have dementia. What is not clear is whether the dementia arises from the same cause as the PD, or whether the two conditions—fairly common in people in their 60s and 70s—occur together by chance. Certainly, some PD cases do have plaques and tangles, as in AD at post-mortem. Certain drugs used to treat the condition have also been blamed for the person's confusion. Depression is quite common, and may also contribute to difficulties of concentration. Some people with other forms of dementia—AD and MID for instance—develop PD at a later stage. This is presumably due to the disorder going on to affect the movement centres below the cortex, having already damaged many important areas within the cortex itself.

Drug treatments are available for PD and, whilst not halting the disease, they can be very helpful in reducing disability. They need to be carefully monitored and supervised in order for the most benefit to be gained.

BOXING

The 'punch-drunk' syndrome still occurs amongst those who subject themselves to repeated blows to the head in the cause of sport (jockeys are also at risk). The first signs are slurred speech and a slowing of movement, with memory problems arising some time later. Again, there are specific areas of the brain that tend to show most damage, with loss of neurons in certain areas. As in AD, neurofibrillary tangles occur, but no plaques are in evidence here.

AIDS

There are reports of loss of memory and general intellectual decline in the final stages of this condition. In part, this may be directly attributed to the virus itself attacking and destroying brain cells; but, it may also be caused by the person's deteriorating physical condition, leading also to problems in the brain. It may be that the intensive research being carried out on this condition will have long-term implications for our knowledge of some of the other dementias.

Alzheimer's Disease

The disease takes its name from a German neurologist, Alois Alzheimer. In 1907 he described the specific changes, now thought to be characteristic of the disease, in the brain of a 51-year-old woman, who had died after a four-and-a-half year loss of ability. These changes can only be seen when various parts of the brain are examined under a microscope. (Obviously, this can only be carried out after the patient's death under normal circumstances.) They have been studied extensively over the last 80 years, although their specific significance remains one of the great mysteries of AD. These changes are:

Plaques

These are found mainly in the outer layer of the brain—the cortex. They are relatively large—often bigger than the largest neurones, but still needing a great deal of magnification before they can be seen. They appear to be made up of an assortment of abnormal, thickened nerve endings. In larger plaques there is a central area, or core, containing fibres of a protein substance called amyloid.

Tangles

In contrast to plaques, neurofibrillary tangles are found *within* one of the most important types of brain cell (the neuron). The tangle consists of a dense bundle of neurofilaments. These tiny fibres normally contribute to the efficient working of the brain cells. The tangles include pairs of filaments wound around one another in a spiral. They are mainly composed of protein, and are similar in some respects to the amyloid found in plaques.

The presence of plaques and tangles have been thought to reflect a decline in brain function, although their exact significance is still being investigated (*see* Chapter 8). It is of interest that they do occur in other, rarer diseases. They are also found—in much smaller quantities—in the brains of elderly people who have died without any dementia being apparent. These 'specific' Alzheimer changes are therefore not quite so specific as it seems! However, generally speaking, it is only in Alzheimer's Disease that large quantities are found in many areas of the cortex. It is usually the case that the more plaques and tangles in the brain, the more severe the person's dementia will have been. The highest density of plaques and tangles are often found in those areas of the cortex particularly responsible for memory and learning functions.

Causes

At present, the cause (or causes) are not known. In Chapter 8 some of the current theories are described.

Risk factors

Can any factors be identified that increase or decrease a person's chances of suffering from AD? Some progress has been made in this area, although as yet no clear ways of preventing AD are apparent. Among the risk factors already identified are:

1   Age—like many disorders, the older a person is the more likely they are to suffer from AD. It is sometimes suggested that once a person reaches their late 80s/early 90s the risk declines again. Unfortunately, it has not proved possible to study a large enough group of such people to establish this for certain. There is also remarkably little evidence to show how common AD is in people under the age of 65.

2   Head injury—relatives of AD sufferers are more likely to report that the person has had a head injury at some time in the past. These injuries may have occurred many years ago. Whether this merely represents an effort by relatives to make sense of the person's disability remains to be seen. As yet we have no idea what proportion of people who are injured in this way go on to develop AD.

3   Family history of AD—the risk of developing AD is increased if one or more close relatives have also suffered from it (see below).

4   Down's Syndrome—people who suffer from Down's Syndrome—a chromosomal abnormality often associated with life-long mental handicap—have a much greater risk of developing AD. Life expectancy is lower than normal, and those who reach their 50s nearly always have plaques and tangles in their brains, and many show a general decline in their abilities.

5   A family history of Down's Syndrome—where there are cases of Down's Syndrome within a family, the risk of AD affecting the person relatively young is increased.

6   A family history of certain other disorders—if there are cases of lymphomas (cancers of the blood) or of thyroid disease in the family, there is again an increased risk of the early onset of AD.

Diagnosis
The first stage in making a diagnosis is to establish the presence of dementia—this is done by excluding other conditions that might produce a similar picture. If there is no evidence that any of these other conditions are present, the next step is to identify what type of dementia the person has. In an older person, if there is no evidence of blood supply problems, AD is the most likely cause. In younger people some of the other conditions also need to be considered. There tend to be small differences in how the person is affected, and in the rate of decline, which enable experienced doctors to make an educated guess as to whether AD is present or not. Definitive diagnosis comes from examination of the brain which is usually possible only after death. In exceptional circumstances it is possible for a surgeon to remove a small piece of brain for examination whilst the person is alive—but until a treatment for AD is available this brain biopsy procedure will seldom be justifiable.

Treatment
No treatment to cure or reverse AD is yet available. A great deal of research is currently under way (see Chapter 8), and it is conceivable that some useful approaches will be identified in the next few years.

Time span
On average, younger patients survive about 6 or 7 years; older patients on average 3 or 4 years. The disease has a greater impact on life-expectancy in the under 65s who, in normal circumstances, would have survived much longer. The range of the duration of the disease can be much wider than these figures suggest—up to 20 years in a few cases.

Is AD hereditary?
'Will I get AD like my mother? Her mother went funny in her old age. What about my children?'
    Unlike Huntington's Disease, AD is not generally thought to be an inherited disease. It is of course very common among older people, so that if your relatives survive into their 70s or 80s there is a good chance that one in five of them will have a form of dementia. It can then be very common for several

members of a long-lived family to suffer from one form of dementia or another. There has been shown to be a slightly increased risk if there are cases of AD in the family—although looking back it is often hard to establish which form of dementia a relative had some years ago. Where the relative has begun to suffer from AD fairly young, the risk of their children eventually suffering from it is increased. The age of onset, however, does not seem to be inherited.

A link with Down's Syndrome has been identified; the risk of AD is increased where there are cases of Down's Syndrome in the family and vice versa. If you are concerned about your own family, and looking back there do seem to be a number of cases of possible AD/Down's Syndrome in close relatives, it is well worth seeking the reassurance of a genetic counsellor. He or she can go through your family tree with you, and help you work out the various risks involved.

What does NOT cause AD

1   Under use of the brain. The disease can affect people who have remained intellectually active, or who are still carrying out intellectually demanding jobs.

2   Over use of the brain. There is no evidence that overwork or 'thinking too much' can cause AD. Overwork can produce lots of other problems—stress, family problems and so on—but it seems impossible literally to wear out your brain cells!

3   AD is not infectious—it cannot be transmitted from one person to another. Living with an AD sufferer may well lead to strain and depression in the carer. Any memory and concentration problems the carer experiences are likely to arise from the stress rather than from AD.

4   AD is not caused by sudden changes such as moving house, a bereavement, a brief admission to hospital, etc. However, this type of event may bring a hidden dementia to light. Whilst the person may be able to cope with the demands of a limited routine, a sudden change often proves too much. On the surface the event appears to 'cause' a sudden onset of dementia; careful investigation, however, usually shows that the problems pre-dated the traumatic event.

5   AD is not caused by 'old age'. Most elderly people in good health retain good memory capacity and are quite capable of learning new skills, learning a new language, finding their way around a new neighbourhood, taking an Open University degree or whatever! Of course, where health problems arise, it is more difficult to think and concentrate intensively. It may well take longer to work things out or to remember a particular event. If you think of memory as a huge filing cabinet, the longer you have been storing the facts away the more there will be, and the longer it will take to find them again. The person with AD has memory problems out of all proportion to the normal variation at any age.

Part of the problem is that we have become so conditioned to expecting these problems as we grow older that any memory lapse over the age of 55 is put down to age. At 25 I burnt a saucepan (more than once)—because I became distracted, was busy, had a lot to think about perhaps . . . If I do the same when I am 75, I will have to be an exceptionally confident person not to blame 'the ageing process'. The fact seems to be that there is not a single ageing process leading downhill. Indeed, age itself is not a very good guide to someone's intellectual abilities. There are, however, a number of diseases that are more likely to hit older people, and these are responsible for many of the difficulties that we so often put down to old age.

Sometimes it is pointed out that we are all losing brain cells from birth. Surely this must have an impact after 70 years or so? It is true that certain brain cells are not replaced —unlike those elsewhere in the body—and so what we are born with is all we will ever have. However, there is more than enough spare capacity to enable us to get through life with little real impairment unless we suffer one of the conditions mentioned above, or our brain is damaged in some other way.

WHY SEEK MEDICAL HELP?

If there's no treatment, why bother seeking medical advice? If there's nothing that can be done, why put the person through tests and investigations? This is a view that seems to be shared by some family doctors. One told a carer: 'I could send your wife up to the M— Hospital, but there's no point. There's nothing they can do for her.'

There are in fact a number of good reasons why every person who is suspected of having AD or any form of dementia should be given a thorough medical examination.

1   A number of other conditions that do respond to treatment may appear quite similar to a dementia or give rise to a dementia-picture. Although these conditions may be rare, each potential AD victim deserves to have them excluded. It is particularly important to make sure the person does not have some physical condition that is interfering with the normal function of the brain. A person of any age who has a fever, is recovering from an anaesthetic or is very ill, may become delirious and lose touch with reality. Older people are more vulnerable to such a state—perhaps because they have less brain power in reserve. They may be delirious when suffering from an infection even though the fever is not raging—as it would have to do in a younger person. They may be affected by doses and combinations of medication, drugs and alcohol that would not have so powerful an effect on a younger person. The problem may grumble on slowly without the obvious signs of illness displayed earlier in life. It may simply be the lack of awareness, the poor memory and perhaps poor speech that are immediately apparent. Identifying one of these 'acute confusional states' is very important. Treating the underlying problem—most commonly a chest or a urine infection—or stopping the drugs that have had untoward effects can lead to the person returning to normal again.

2   Depression is a fairly common condition at any age. In its severest forms, when the person withdraws into an inner world of blackness and suffering, she may appear lost and confused and lose all interest in personal appearance and hygiene. When asked the standard questions—'What day is it today? Who is the Prime Minister? What's the name of this place?' she may well give no answer at all or a careless, mistaken one to end the questioning. At this level of depression the person may actually appear to have dementia. Correct diagnosis is essential because unlike

dementia, severe depression responds well to treatment and fairly effective measures are available, including anti-depressant drugs and electro-convulsive therapy.

To complicate matters further, some people who are developing dementia are also (understandably) depressed. Specialist help is needed to sort out all these possibilities. In the past there have been instances of patients who have been admitted to permanent hospital care with 'severe dementia' some years previously, and later discharged when a proper evaluation is carried out and their depression treated. This is an awful mistake to make— especially when you consider the anguish and suffering of a person undergoing a severe depression without the help they need to recover.

3   Even if the diagnosis is AD or another form of dementia it can be helpful to know what you are dealing with. It assists planning for the future; it helps you to come to terms with what is happening to your relative. At last you can blame a disease, rather than the person you love, for their odd behaviour, their awkwardness, and even their aggression.

4   Medical evaluation may open the door to a number of other useful services and facilities—day-care, periods of holiday relief, even financial assistance (the attendance allowance in the UK, for example). The medical team may include other professionals who can offer different sorts of help, for example an occupational therapist to advise on aids to make caring easier, a social worker to give information on benefits and services. Various team members will be able to lend a listening ear and offer support and advice as the caring continues.

5   The various services can get to know you and the sufferer before a crisis develops. This can make it easier to plan the 'sharing of the caring' that is vital for the carer's well-being. The person may need medical care and possibly medication during the course of the disorder. By establishing a good relationship with a medical team, you have a better chance of getting the help you will need when you need it, and of having any physical problems the person may develop treated seriously and sympathetically. A good medical ally is well worth having, and having a full

medical evaluation as early as possible is a good way of developing a helpful partnership.

6 There may be more than one disorder going on at once, for example the person may have both AD and an acute confusional state (perhaps arising from a urine infection). The secondary process may be treatable, and the happy result will be an improvement in the person's overall condition.

7 Finally, a reason with less immediate benefit: it will help increase knowledge of AD and other disorders if they are followed through from early on in the condition. Better help and advice may then be available for future sufferers and their carers.

WHO SHOULD CARRY OUT THE MEDICAL EVALUATION?

They will need a knowledge of and an interest in AD and its related conditions and access to some investigative facilities. The right person could be a neurologist, a psychiatrist, a geriatrician or a psychogeriatrician, depending on how old the person is and how much incapacity he/she has (see table 1). Much will depend on how well services are developed and organised in your area—if you are able to get in touch with other carers locally, they may be able to advise where they have found the most help.

Table 1:   The Professionals

Neurologist	a medical doctor who specialises in disorders of the brain and of the nerve pathways
Psychiatrist	a medical doctor specialising in mental illnesses
Geriatrician	a medical doctor specialising in the illnesses afflicting elderly people
Psychogeriatrician	a psychiatrist, specialising in mental illnesses in elderly people
Clinical Psychologist	a non-medical specialist on the brain's memory, learning and other functions

Most family doctors probably would not be able to undertake this task. Although AD is commonly encountered, few GPs have the time to acquire the specialised knowledge required—they encounter so many different conditions that it is hard for them to have specialised knowledge of more than a few. Many carers report having to teach their GP about AD!

You will need medical assistance at various points, so it is important to identify sources of help where you feel that the sufferer's condition is taken seriously, where time is taken to explain to you what is happening, and where you are involved in any decisions being taken.

Different centres adopt different methods for their assessment procedures—a brief admission to hospital, a series of out-patient appointments, or a sequence of visits, perhaps two or three times a week, to a day-hospital. The assessment itself will probably include the following:

An interview with someone who knows the person well to establish the background to the condition, how and when it emerged. This is helpful in considering whether the person may be suffering from depression, or be in an acute confusional state, or, more generally, in giving ideas as to what form of dementia might be present.

Details of the person's medical history, including any previous psychiatric problems.

A full physical examination to identify any contributory physical problems. Reflexes, hearing and eye-sight will be tested, blood pressure taken and weight measured.

Blood tests—to exclude vitamin deficiencies, thyroid problems, certain infections, etc.

An interview with the patient, which will include an assessment of their mood to see if there is a significant level of depression. The person will also be asked some simple questions to test their knowledge of current events, awareness of their whereabouts, and their ability to learn new information. The interview will give some indication of whether the person is aware of any difficulties, and how they see their situation.

Chest X-ray—gives some indications of chest infections, heart and lung disorders that may be contributing to the person's problems.

Urine testing—may give indications of infection or diabetes. In addition there may also be:

EEG (Electroencephalogram)—in this procedure small electrodes are fixed to the person's head with special adhesive, and a recording made of the person's 'brain waves'—the electrical activity of the brain. In AD, there is a slowing down of electrical activity. If a person has been having fits, the EEG can often indicate roughly where in the brain the problem lies. The procedure seems a little odd at first, particularly to a patient who lacks awareness or understanding of what is happening, and it involves the person lying still for a few minutes whilst the recording is being made. However, it is not at all dangerous or harmful, and the main cause of discomfort comes in removing the adhesive from the person's hair (try nail varnish remover!).

ECG (Electrocardiogram)—this is a very common, simple procedure which gives a recording of the person's heart function from electrodes attached to the person's chest.

Neuropsychological testing—sometimes the person will be seen by a clinical psychologist for a more detailed assessment of their memory capacity, learning and other abilities. These tests are quite time-consuming and can also be a little stressful if the person is aware of her failings, but the psychologist will make every effort to reduce the person's anxiety and stress. Some of the latest tests are based on video-games, the patient interacting with a small computer that monitors her performance. Most psychologists will be delighted to discuss the results of the tests with the carer.

CT Scan (Computerised Tomography)—this is a sophisticated form of X-ray that uses computer technology to build up a picture of the brain at different levels. It can detect brain shrinkage or any large infarcts that may be present. It will also reveal any growth (or tumour) in the brain, which could of course be causing problems. The procedure involves the person lying on an X-ray table with the head inside a circular hole, around which is the scanning apparatus. The scanner resembles a washing machine, and some patients may need reassurance about this. They have to remain still while the scan takes place (it usually lasts about 10 minutes). Sometimes it is advisable to have a person familiar with the patient present so that he can be made to feel more secure and relaxed. Again, it is not in any way a harmful procedure, and it is very helpful in understanding the person's problems. The CT scanner is very expensive, and so is not available in every centre.

PET scan (Positron Emission Tomography)—even more expensive than CT scans, but allows for a more detailed examination of areas of interest in the brain. Whilst the CT scan indicates the structure of the person's brain, the PET scan shows the activity within the various brain areas, and how it is reduced in the parts of the brain most affected. The scanning takes rather longer than a CT scan. At present it is available in very few centres.

A definitive diagnosis cannot always be made immediately; it may take some months to rule out every possibility. AD is diagnosed by excluding other possible causes; none of the various investigations and tests can prove that AD is present. Only after the person's death can the diagnosis be proved conclusively, although in most cases the diagnosis becomes reasonably secure over a period of time.

The Symptoms of Dementia

When carers get together and start discussing the problems they have encountered, it is quite common for one to say to another, 'No that can't be AD—in AD they ...'. In other words, comparisons are made, and very different patterns of disability and disturbance emerge. Naturally enough, the assumption is made that the two people under discussion cannot be suffering from the same condition. The reality is that we are considering here a group of varied conditions which do hit different people in sometimes quite diverse ways. An important consequence is that it is difficult to predict exactly how the person's condition will change and develop over time. How quickly will the person deteriorate? How bad will it become? These are important questions which cannot always be answered satisfactorily because:

1   we are dealing with several different disorders;
2   even within AD there are probably different sub-types of the disorder;

3   there is a random element to the damage that occurs in MID, and possibly to some extent in AD;
4   in a progressive disorder people will naturally be at different stages;
5   people of different ages are often affected differently by the same disease—many disorders are less devastating in older people where the disease progresses more slowly. This seems to be true of AD.
6   People respond differently to disease and disability—they react to it and try to cope with it. But here the coping system is itself amongst the casualties of the disease. This makes coping and adjustment more difficult and accentuates the differences between individuals.
7   People differ greatly in their physical health and other physical conditions co-existing with the dementia.

There is then a great deal of variation between patients. What *can* be said with certainty?

First, the person will have undergone some changes—in memory, learning ability, the capacity to work things out or make sensible plans. Secondly, the person will generally get worse, and be less able to look after themselves. In younger patients this deterioration may be obvious within a few months, with a progression to a very severe degree of impairment in a couple of years. In older patients, the decline may be over a ten-year period. Other features tend not to be so universal. It is helpful to divide them into those likely to occur early on in the condition, those occurring when the disorder is well-established, and those most likely to be present in the final stages.

EARLY FEATURES

It is difficult to pinpoint exactly when AD begins because of its gradual onset. Perhaps some of the features are evident only when looking back—at the time they may have been attributed to the person getting old, being difficult, or just being their old selves but more so! A lot depends on the sort of life the person is living and the demands being made upon them. For instance, someone doing a job which places a lot of demands on memory may well show difficulties before somebody who has retired and lives a quiet, undemanding life. Someone who regularly plays a game like bridge, where good memory is essential, may be noticed by their regular partners to be doing less well. In other situations there may just be increasing memory lapses, repeated conversations, odd moments where the person seems puzzled and perplexed. Early on these signs may be attributed to depression or anxiety, lack of interest in work or hobbies, tiredness; or put down to increasing pressure, stress or worries. This is perfectly understandable—all these factors can lead to similar mild problems of concentration and memory.

Often the person's work-mates, or a close relative if in the home, reduce the impact of the problems by 'carrying' the person, taking on some of the responsibilities or duties they can no longer manage, and perhaps not really registering that a serious problem is developing at all. This process may occur quite unconsciously if the changes are gradual—only looking back does it all become clear. Table 2 shows the experience of a large number of carers of the earliest indications that something was amiss.

Table 2: the earliest symptoms

Memory loss, disorientation	62%
Problems with work	20%
Changes in personality	19%
Generally unable to function	15%
Physical changes	13%
Problems with driving	13%
Difficulty in managing money	12%

Based on a sample survey of 284 carers.

Adapted from Chenoweth & Spencer, 1986; Gerontologist, pp. 267–272.

The person may be less adaptable, becoming excessively upset at small changes of routine, coping badly with a holiday, for example that would in previous years have been taken in his stride. Perhaps aware of this, the person may be reluctant to try new things or visit new places. Indeed, sometimes a gradual withdrawal from previous social ties and interests may occur, with the person perhaps unwittingly taking this action to prevent the embarrassment of social failure. The more complex and demanding the situation, the more likely it is to bring the person's problems to the surface.

The person may try to make sense of what is happening to them by becoming more involved with themselves and their own feelings, showing less concern for and being less sensitive to the needs of others. At times they may become irritated at what would seem to be small mistakes or minor frustrations, but which in the context of AD may be yet another instance of failing powers. Some people may cope with this by becoming quite defensive, denying any difficulties and even blaming others for things that get mislaid. Some people will take this as far as accusing others of stealing their possessions. The alternative explanation—a simple lapse in memory—cannot be accepted.

Oddly enough, it may be friends and relatives who don't see the person very often who may spot the changes first—the person who sees them most may be too close to recognise such gradual changes. A person living alone may forget to send birthday cards for the first time for years, or may forget details of family events. Where the person lives with the carer, the carer may be so effectively filling the gaps that nobody else notices. Much depends on the sort of relationship enjoyed in the past and the way in which various duties were shared between the people involved.

THE PROBLEM DEVELOPS

The typical problems related to dementia are becoming apparent. The person fails to remember details of everyday life; she often repeats herself and finds it hard to remember the names of people and things. She may get lost whilst out walking—particularly on less familiar routes. Saucepans are often left to boil dry in the kitchen. Skills begin to be lost, whether it be in the kitchen, the workshop or the office. Only the most generous of employers will allow the younger AD sufferer to continue in employment. Even the most helpful of work-mates will find it difficult to 'carry' the person as the problems worsen. If the person still drives a car, vehicle control will be noticeably worse.

There will be some fluctuations, of course. The person may

wake one morning as if in a daze, asking for a family member who left home years previously, or believing they have to get the children to school; the children (now in their 50s) may dispute this, only to find that they have been mistaken for someone else. At other times recent events are soon forgotten while events of years gone by seem to be recalled vividly. Repetitions become more and more frequent—the needle is stuck on the damaged record.

The person may begin to do dangerous things. Some of these may be caused by poor memory and lack of concentration. A gas tap may be left on, possibly unlit; the sufferer may lock himself out of the house. Others seem more related to a loss of judgement and common sense—crossing the road carelessly, letting strangers into the house, putting down lighted matches or cigarettes, carelessly drying clothes over an open flame on a gas-cooker, going outside in inadequate clothing.

Time may become a problem. Sometimes day and night may become reversed, with the person wanting to go shopping in the middle of the night and sleep all day. Or days may become mixed up—the person may turn up for an appointment on the wrong day or wonder why no one else was at the church on a Wednesday. Meal-times may be forgotten, or another meal requested immediately after a good lunch!

The person may have lots of energy and considerable determination. Having gone out and perhaps got lost they may keep on walking for hours—apparently in the hope of coming across something familiar. It is not uncommon for someone to find their way back to a street where they lived many years previously. It is amazing how far some AD sufferers can go with no money in their pockets, and sometimes still in their slippers!

If the person lives alone, hygiene and feeding may be neglected—perhaps forgotten about altogether. The person may tell visitors most indignantly that they have had a bath or a meal when the evidence is clear that they have not!

Sometimes the person may see or hear things that aren't present—small children playing in the house, for example, or strangers sitting on the armchairs. This may be a frightening experience depending on their interpretation of what they have perceived. The person's reaction to what is happening will once again colour the problems seen. There may be accusations or anger when challenged, or the person may become distressed very rapidly.

AS THE PROBLEMS BECOME SEVERE. . .

As time goes on the person is likely to need help and supervision in more and more areas of life. She may need help with dressing; she may put on her clothes in the wrong order (a vest over a dress, for example) or not be able to put them on at all. Feeding skills may deteriorate and table manners be lost, the person using a spoon or fingers inappropriately. Washing and bathing may need close supervision to ensure they are actually carried out with any degree of thoroughness. The person may need help going to the toilet. She may begin to have accidents—a wet bed may be discovered at night; then, later on, accidents may occur during the day. Incontinence of faeces is less common, but it does occur in a number of patients. Some patients' walking deteriorates, and others become almost completely immobile.

By this time memory is very poor indeed—the person will probably not be aware of the time of day, the day of the week or the year; they may not know their address, or even be certain of the identities of the people around them. They may get lost even in the familiar surroundings of their own home, and certainly in anywhere unfamiliar. Repetitions become more and more frequent—sometimes a few phrases or sounds may be repeated constantly. Relatives will frequently not be recognised, or mistaken for other people. There will be considerable uncertainty about which *phase* of life the person is in. Are the children still at home? Shouldn't I be at work? Will my mother be here soon? Confusions of this kind may be apparent. The person may have great difficulty making sense of what is happening roundabout, not seeming to recognise objects or unable to grasp even fairly simple conversation. Communication becomes increasingly difficult, and eventually the person's speech may make little sense.

Sometimes particular problems arise. The person may be very restless, full of energy which is difficult to direct constructively. A particular idea—looking for a purse, a pension book or a relative who has moved away, for example—may become fixed and difficult to shift, even when reassurances are given that the object or the person is in safe keeping. Night-time may become a problem; agitation may seem to increase as it approaches. The person may place more reliance on light and dark as indicators of time than the clock—if it's dark, it's time for bed; if light, it must be time to get up! Some sufferers seem to lose their inhibitions, taking off their clothes in front of other people, or using a waste-paper bin as a toilet, for example; or they may shout and scream for no apparent reason. Aggressive incidents may occur, especially when the person feels hemmed in or pressurised by those around them. Occasionally AD sufferers may have epileptic fits, losing consciousness and jerking uncontrollably.

MEMORY

As we have already seen, changes in memory are amongst the most commonly reported 'first signs' of AD, and at each stage memory problems of increasing severity will be amongst the key features. A dementia without memory problems is almost unheard of, yet there are a variety of other difficulties. Some of these other problems could simply be a result of poor memory—forgetting to have a bath regularly, for example; forgetting what stage they have reached in a complex sequential task such as getting dressed, and so putting on clothes in the wrong order; forgetting what the time is and going out, say, to the shops in the middle of the night. In many AD sufferers there is a genuine loss of skill over and above the memory problems, so that practical tasks become difficult even if help *is* given with sequencing. The person may still fail to grasp the connection between different elements of a task or lack judgement.

Some patients do suffer from memory problems (or amnesia alone); their problems are great, but in many ways these people remain more intact than the AD sufferer who also has difficulties reasoning and thinking. The film director Luis Bunuel is quoted by Sacks[1] as saying: 'Life without memory is

[1] See Appendix

no life at all ... Our memory is our coherence, our reason, our feeling, even our action. Without it we are nothing ...' Sacks argues in fact that, even without memory, spiritual awareness and emotional sensitivity are possible; the wider-ranging damage inflicted by AD makes it all the harder to hold on to what Sacks describes as 'the undiminished possibility of reintegration by art, by communion, by touching the human spirit.'

Many AD sufferers have difficulty naming pictures of fairly common objects; partly, they forget the exact name-label that goes with a particular object; but there can also be difficulties in recognising the object—what it is and what it is used for. Similarly, there may be problems in recognising people's names and faces. When this extends to the person's immediate family, this can be most distressing—the sufferer no longer even recognises who they are. One patient only recognised her husband of 50 years as such when he wore his trilby hat. He said how odd it felt having to go to bed in his hat—but it was the only way his wife would let him into the bedroom!

Many families notice that whilst the sufferer is quite unable to recall what he had for lunch 10 minutes ago, he seems able to remember the happenings of 60 years ago perfectly. And yet when this has been tested systematically—the remembered events checked against factual sources, for example—the picture is less reassuring. The sufferer may be skilled at repeating well rehearsed and often repeated tales, but his knowledge of actual fact is much more hazy. This is akin to the way many of us remember the words of songs or poetry—at some time or another we repeated them so often that they became second nature to us.

PERSONALITY

The loss of memory and other abilities takes away much of what makes the person who they are. However, it is patently obvious that not all AD sufferers are the same. Some are delightfully polite and sociable, making small talk to perfect strangers as if they were old family friends. Others are moody and irritable, or suspicious and wary of any but the most familiar faces. Some always seem to have a smile, others appear gloomy and miserable. Some are lively and active, inquisitive and curious; others are apathetic and withdrawn. To what extent do these differences reflect the life-long personality styles of these individuals? Or is it just a reflection of the different way AD affects different people? By and large, the saying 'To have a sweet old lady you must first have a sweet young lady' seems to hold true. People become less complex in their personalities, but there seems to be continuity in their basic approach to life. There are, as ever, exceptions to this. Some individuals undergo a drastic personality change—they lose social control, doing and saying things that would once have seemed outrageous. Often this is related to damage suffered by the frontal areas of the brain, areas which are thought to help us maintain our normal inhibitions. Thus a previously quiet, demure lady, a former Sunday School teacher perhaps, begins to swear like a trooper; or a man who has previously been very upright, a 'real gentleman', starts to make improper suggestions to female patients at the day-centre.

Another factor that can lead to an apparent 'about-turn' in personality is that AD presents a terrible challenge—the person is forced to cope and survive at a level never experienced before. Being in a totally new situation, where the demands outstrip failing resources and abilities, the person responds uncharacteristically. One wife, for example described how upset she was when for the first time in 40 years of marriage, her husband hit her. One way of looking at this situation would be to say that the husband's personality had changed—once placid and gentle, he was now angry and aggressive. A more subtle observer would remark that the husband had never had to be helped to go to the toilet before. He could no longer deal with his anger at his lack of self-control in an appropriate way—by talking it through with his wife or letting off steam in some other way. Dementia had taken away these options too, and so in this totally unprecedented situation, an apparently 'out of character' reaction occurred.

Personality changes of this kind may occur then, but, in general, the person's basic demeanour will be preserved, albeit in a more simple, primitive form, until the disabilities become so extensive that it is almost impossible to recognise the person's residual personality.

DOES THE PERSON HAVE INSIGHT?

Many carers are obviously concerned to know how much the sufferer understands of what is happening. Relatives frequently reassure themselves that at least their loved one is unaware of the deterioration in so many aspects of their lives, a fact that is only too clear to those looking on. But does the sufferer have *any* awareness of her condition? Most text-books of psychiatry and neurology would affirm that the AD sufferer has no insight into her own condition. This is probably true in the general sense that the person rarely says, 'I suffer from Alzheimer's Disease, which affects my memory and other abilities'.

A few years ago I would have said this never occurs. Recently, however, I have become aware of people who have shown this degree of awareness at an early stage in the development of their condition. As public awareness of the disorder grows, it is likely that many other people will use the label AD to 'explain' certain lapses of concentration and memory. Some will be mistaken, of course—a large proportion of people complaining of memory and concentration difficulties turn out to be simply depressed but others, sadly will be correct in their suspicions. The very nature of the disease is likely to keep the proportion of sufferers who are able to name and have some knowledge of their condition relatively small. These people will of course need particular support and help in coming to terms with such a threatening process.

A much larger group of sufferers is vaguely aware that something is wrong, although the level of this awareness may vary a great deal. A surprising number will accept the doctor's gentle suggestion that perhaps their memory is not quite as good as it used to be. One lady whose impairment was very severe, to the extent that it was often hard to understand what she was saying, suddenly said very clearly one day, 'My brain's gone'. Such flashes of awareness make it difficult to know just how much or how little the sufferer understands of her plight.

For those who do not suffer such impairment, it is hard to imagine what awareness would be like. It is helpful to remember that each of us, when faced with a severe stress, a disability or a difficulty of some kind, tries to cope with it in some way or another. We try to reduce the impact of the stress on our lives in order to make it seem less awful and overwhelming. Successful coping results in coming to terms with the stress or the loss that has been sustained, perhaps compensating as much as possible for what has been lost. Failure to find ways of coping results in increasing distress and despair. With any loss, distress and sadness are almost inevitable to some extent, and accordingly, are very common also in the early stages of AD. Early on some sufferers will be able to develop practical strategies and techniques for minimising their losses, perhaps placing greater reliance on memory aids (a diary, for example) that were previously useful, but which now become essential prompts. Others will reduce their range of activities to minimise the demands being made upon them—the less one attempts the less one is likely to fail. Social gatherings—like a regular card playing session—will be dropped as memory problems interfere with the person's ability to play at his previous level. Others cope with stress by blaming others for what has happened. For such people it seems to be less distressing to assume that if a favourite purse or handbag cannot be found someone else—the home-help, a neighbour, a relative even—has stolen it than to entertain even for a moment the thought that there could possibly be something wrong within themselves, even a failure of memory. Others will deny the existence of any problem—even if the evidence is only too clear. They may deny, for example, that they have wet their trousers—and even deny that they are wet! Or they may blame someone else or some other cause, saying, for example, that they have spilled their drink. Others, without such a powerful defensive system, break down in the face of obvious failure, collapsing into tears or lashing out aggressively in response to the frustration and humiliation of failure.

In other words, full awareness of AD would be for most people a threat to their very existence, an inconceivable assault on their integrity; and some of the reactions commonly seen in

AD sufferers may be viewed as a reaction to, or a defence against, such awareness. Most sufferers do seem to find some way of coping with the enormity of the disability; of reducing the distress and anxiety that is so often encountered in the early changes of the disorder. Some will continue to feel threatened or frustrated by their environment; for them, it is not so much their awareness of their condition that is a problem as their inability to make sense of what is happening to them.

Chapter Two

Every carer has a story...

In a book such as this information is given in general terms, and it can often be difficult to see how it might be applied to a specific situation. This chapter aims to redress the balance by recounting a number of carers' experiences of the disease—its beginnings, its progression and its impact upon their lives. No single story can be typical or representative, the accounts selected illustrate as wide a range of experiences as possible. Each one is a composite of several real-life accounts, and some details have been changed to preserve the often confidential nature of what carers have shared with me.

A daughter's tale

When did you first notice something was wrong with your mother?
It was about three years ago, after dad died. At first we thought it was just that she was missing him so much—after all, they had been married over 50 years and they were always together. They really lived for each other. We used to think dad did too much for mum. Nothing was too much trouble for him. When she kept phoning up in a state, often asking something we'd already talked about, I thought she was playing up, trying to get me to run around for her like dad did. Looking back, I wonder whether dad was covering up her problems by helping her so much—he never said anything was wrong, but he wasn't the sort to complain. I feel guilty now because at first I was really hard on mum. I was determined she was not going to become dependent on me. Of course, we were all upset about dad's death, but I thought mum should be able to get on with life like the rest of us had to. Now I realise

that this awful disease was even then taking hold, I wish I'd been more sympathetic.

When did you discover what was causing the problems?
When I realised that mum really was forgetting things from one day to the next, and that she wasn't aware of the way she was neglecting herself, I suggested she come with me to her family doctor for a check up. She refused, so I rang the doctor myself. He said there was nothing he could do unless mum went to see him—even though she was 78 by that time. I tried Social Services. They arranged meals on wheels and a home help, so at least I knew she would be getting a meal and having some help with the housework. It was when she was found wandering in the street in her night-clothes that the doctor had to take some action. He arranged for a doctor from the hospital to see her at home; luckily I was there when he came or mum would never have let him in the house. He asked her a few questions—what day was it, who was the Prime Minister, that sort of thing—and tested her memory by asking her to remember a few things. Then he came into the kitchen and spoke to me on my own. I really appreciated that. I couldn't talk about mum, and let him know what had been happening, in front of her could I? He said that she would have some more tests, but it was virtually certain she was suffering from dementia. He said she could have the tests at the day-hospital, so that she wouldn't actually need to go into hospital. I had my doubts whether she would agree to go anywhere near that hospital because it still has the reputation round here of being somewhere you don't come out from! But it was obviously worth a try, and the doctor seemed really helpful and understanding.

Had you come across the term dementia before?
No, not really. I knew some old people become senile; and my husband's grandmother went into a home because her memory was completely gone—but we didn't have much contact with her. They lived quite a long way away. But it took me a while to understand more about dementia being an illness. It was much later before I heard the term 'Alzheimer's Disease' and realised mum had got it. The psychiatrist who visited her at home did try to explain a bit about dementia, but it was difficult as mum kept calling for me—she must have known we

were talking about her. He told me her condition would probably get worse; that she would need a lot of help and would probably eventually have to go into a home or hospital. I can remember him saying those things, but they didn't sink in — it was like being in a state of shock. I wanted to believe she would get better. I just could not accept at first that my mum would never be the same again. But as the tests confirmed the diagnosis of dementia, and no other cause was found, I've had to face the fact that it isn't going to go away. I still hope something might turn up—a new cure even—and some days I think she is more like her old self, but I know deep down that I'm clutching at straws. It's final, definite, and all I can hang onto are the memories of mum as she used to be and those fleeting glimpses of her old self. I feel very sad about it, but there it is—I have to accept it.

Has your mother's condition deteriorated rapidly?
Well, her memory certainly gets worse and worse, though now we expect it to be bad, whereas at first we were surprised when she forgot something after a few minutes. But compared to some others I've heard about at the carers' group I attend, she's not too far along the road to decline. She's only been incontinent a few times, and she's never really been aggressive. She can still get around all right and she can even do some jobs —like drying-up the dishes or ironing—if we watch her. She is quite vulnerable though, and a cold or a change of routine can make her much worse quite suddenly; when the day-centre is closed on one of her usual days she gets upset and agitated. She seems to know she ought to be going somewhere, although she doesn't know what day it is or the name of the centre.

You mentioned a day-centre. What help have you received?
The hospital arranged for her to attend a day-centre. It's run by Social Services, I think. It has been a real life-saver. She goes there three days a week now. When she's there I know she's safe and being well looked after, so I can relax and not worry so much about her. The staff there are very helpful. In fact, they're marvellous with her—they even get her to join in some of the activities. She has a good lunch there, though she'll come back and say she's had nothing to eat at her 'club'. She sleeps well after her days there—I think it must help, keeping her

more occupied. A few times the transport hasn't arrived to take her, and if I hadn't been able to get away from work, it would have been difficult. But usually it works out. She still has a home help to do most of the cleaning for her, and meals on wheels on the weekdays she's not at the centre. She doesn't always eat them (sometimes I've found them in the bin untouched, and at other times in even odder places—like the wardrobe!). She doesn't pay much attention to personal cleanliness these days, so we asked for a bath attendant to visit and help her have a bath once a week. She didn't like that at all — she told the poor lady where to go in no uncertain terms! We were really embarrassed, but there wasn't anything we could do. Now we just encourage her to have a good wash, but her personal hygiene certainly leaves something to be desired. The social worker suggested we apply for an Attendance Allowance. It took ages to come through, but now we spend it on having a carer from an agency coming in two evenings a week to sit with her, keep her company, give her her sleeping tablets and get her settled for bed. Without the tablets she gets up in the middle of the night and goes out, expecting the shops to be open. So far she's never got too lost, but her sense of direction is getting worse and worse. At least I have two evenings a week to myself now.

Although you don't actually live with your mother, you're obviously very involved with her care. What exactly do you do for her at the moment?
I go round there each morning and make sure she's up and ready for the day-centre transport on three days or for the home-help the other two days. I have to make sure she changes her clothes at least sometimes, which can mean removing the clothes she's been wearing—I have to do that very stealthily— and taking them away to be washed. I get her some breakfast, and make sure she has her morning pills (for her thyroid, I think). Then I go off to work—it's a part-time job and, luckily, very flexible, but without it I'd probably crack up completely. Then around 4 o'clock I go round again, make her some tea, and take back any laundry I've done for her. Then after I've prepared a meal at home for my husband, son and myself, it's back to mum's for a couple of hours to settle her for the night.

That's except for Mondays and Fridays, which are my nights off! At weekends she spends most of the day and evening with us. Of course, we have to handle all her finances for her now, and all the repairs and redecoration to her house. Life can be very hectic! My son, who is now in his thirties, is mentally handicapped and attends a special centre each day—he needs a lot of attention as well.

You must feel very stretched. How do you cope?
Sometimes it really is difficult. I could scream sometimes. I go round to her and she says, 'What are you doing here? My daughter will be back in a moment'. And I say, 'But I am your daughter!' Then she says, 'Of course you are, dear', and I wonder whether she really didn't recognise me or whether she was just winding me up. Or when we have friends round and she eats her food really messily. She used to be so careful before all this happened—now I find myself apologising for her, and I feel awful. When I get really worked up with her, I pop out for a walk or go home and listen to my favourite music—just to unwind. My husband has been a great help, a tower of strength. I feel guilty sometimes for neglecting him and my son, but he's tremendously understanding. Mum likes him a lot—she's much nicer to him than she is to me! He calms me down when I get uptight, and he insisted I carry on working when I thought it would be easier to give it up. My job is really important; I can really forget everything else while I'm there — I'm totally absorbed. I'm really lucky to have a job and such an understanding partner. I know from my carers' group that not everyone is so fortunate. Having someone to talk to, to let off steam with, is so important. The carers' group helps with that too; the people there really understand what I'm going through, and they've given us lots of ideas about different things to try with mum. One of the carers told me about the agency which provides the evening carers. That's such a help. I do get down sometimes, but then I remember what mum did for me when I was little, and that helps me carry on. I just want to return the kindness she gave me.

Have you had any help from the rest of your family?
That's a sore point I'm afraid. My two brothers have really left it all to me—as if it's my job because I'm the only daughter! It

makes my blood boil to think about it. Admittedly, one of them lives a long way away, but he hardly ever rings, and the one who lives locally hasn't lifted a finger to help. It took ages before they would accept there was anything wrong with mum—they thought I was exaggerating! The local brother did pop in and see her when we had a weekend away last year, but that was only because my husband really made a big issue of it. They could visit or give us a break occasionally, but they give the impression they want to remember mum as she was, not as she is now. The really annoying thing is that mum is always saying how wonderful her boys are! I've got a daughter with two young children, but they live abroad so they can't be of much practical help. When she's home she does a lot and mum loves to see the little children, although I'm sure she doesn't realise she's a great-grandmother!

You had a weekend away last year. Have you had any longer breaks?
A couple of years ago we took mum on holiday with us—it was a disaster; she was so confused away from her familiar surroundings. My brothers won't take her, so we'd have to get a lot more help for her at home or find a place for her in a home if we wanted to go away on our own. The social worker says there is a home that would take her, but I'm worried that the upheaval would confuse her even more. I think next summer we'll have to try something; we're all getting to the point where we really need a holiday. Ideally, we'd love to visit my daughter and her family abroad but, apart from the expense, it's not worth going for less than a month, so that seems an impossibility for the present.

What about the future? Would you consider your mother being placed permanently in residential care?
I've thought about this more and more recently. I want to keep mum in her own home as long as possible, but I know it's going to get more and more difficult. We did think about having her to live with us, but after we'd tried it for a week we could see she needed the familiarity of her own place, and the tensions just mounted so quickly when we were all under the same roof. I've spoken to other carers and they've recommended some good residential homes. Some are fairly close by. Mum would hate the idea of going into a home, but I'm hoping

when it comes to it she will accept it, as she's accepted other help eventually. If she goes into a home for a couple of weeks while we're on holiday, it will at least give us some idea of her reactions. I know that if it comes to that I shall feel awfully guilty, but I'd rather face that than become a complete wreck myself, running round in circles trying to keep mum in her own home. My husband and son need me too.

If only she could tell me what she wants ...

What were the first signs that something was wrong with your wife?
I first noticed a change after Doris retired. She had gone on working past her retirement age, but when I retired she gave up her job as well. She had always coped so well with everything—her job in the solicitor's office, keeping our home beautifully, and all her other outside interests ... She was really active—charity work, that sort of thing. But after she retired she just seemed to lose interest. She seemed to prefer to stay in rather than go out to meetings or socialise. At first I thought it was me, being around too much, being in the way. But we had always planned to do so many things together when we both retired. When it came to it she seemed apathetic, not at all enthusiastic about the plans we had made. She would explain it by saying, 'I just want to take it easy, I've retired now'; but this was out of character for her. I didn't mind taking on the shopping and the cooking and gradually more and more on the domestic side—I needed to occupy myself after a busy working life, and Doris did deserve a rest after all she had done for me and our family over the years. It's only now, looking back, that I realise she was withdrawing into herself because she could no longer cope with the sort of life we had enjoyed up till then.

How long ago was this?
Just coming up to four years—it seems incredible our life could change so much in such a short space of time. She's nearly 68 now, a year younger than myself. We had everything to live for—a comfortable home, lots of time, lovely children and

grand-children, good friends, marvellous holidays. Now we live from day-to-day, managing as best we can. Then we looked forward to the future, now I try not to think about it.

What are the main difficulties your wife has now?
The main ones? It's more a total loss; there's nothing she can do for herself now. Even her walking is deteriorating; apparently she's got Parkinson's Disease as well as Alzheimer's. She's had several falls, so I have to walk with her everywhere now. I have to wash her, dress and undress her, take her to the toilet and more or less feed her. Most days I have to change her clothes at least once—when I don't get her to the toilet in time. You see she can't tell me when she needs the toilet—these days very little of what she says makes any sense at all. I can make some of it out, the odd word, or if she points to something; but most of the time she makes lots of noise, repeating something over and over again sometimes, a word or a bit of nonsense. If only she could tell me what she wants, I could look after her so much better, and we both wouldn't get so frustrated by my inability to understand her.

Has it been a gradual decline? And has it become increasingly difficult for you to cope as your wife's carer?
Yes, the decline has been gradual over the past four years, although she seemed to go downhill more rapidly after her first fall when she broke her wrist. After that I really had to dress and feed her, and she never recovered her abilities after the fracture had mended. I'm not sure caring gets more difficult as time goes on. There's a lot to do now, but I can cope with the physical side of caring; probably a lot of men couldn't do what I do, but my wife means everything to me, and I feel I owe her all the kindness and attention I can give her. There were some tricky patches earlier on when she wasn't nearly so disabled which I found really difficult to cope with. At times she didn't recognise me; I would come home from the shops and she would say, 'Who are you? You'd better watch out, my husband will be back in a minute.' Or she would ask me, 'Where's John?', and I would say, 'I'm John, your husband.' Sometimes she would say, 'Oh, there you are', and everything would be fine. Other times she wouldn't accept me at all.

Sometimes she would become really angry and aggressive to the point of hitting me—some of her language was quite a revelation. I didn't know she knew such words. She'd certainly never used them before all this happened. I must admit there were times when I lost my temper with her. You can't just sit back and take abuse, especially when you're feeling upset, hurt and rejected by the person you love and care for—especially when she doesn't even recognise you as her husband any more! Afterwards I felt so wretched and awful at having lost control, although she seemed to forget the whole thing very quickly indeed. Even though it was always provoked, I still feel guilty about those times when my temper snapped. Perhaps I thought I could shake some sense into her, convince her that I really was her husband; perhaps I hadn't really accepted that it wasn't her fault, that it was an illness; I just wish now that I had been calmer and more able to cope. Now I don't get so angry; I'm more resigned to it, I suppose. In those days it all happened so quickly and unexpectedly. There was the time she came running out of the living room, saying there were men with guns coming after her; I nearly panicked as well till I realised she'd been watching a film on TV. She thought the violent characters on the screen were actually in our living room! I solved the problem that time by turning off the TV, and making sure she didn't watch it alone again. It was only when I met other carers that I discovered that other people had similar experiences. I thought I was the only one, forever coming up against the unexpected.

You mentioned your wife had both Parkinson's and Alzheimer's Diseases. When did you find out what was wrong?
It was after the first occasion she didn't recognise me that I took her to our GP. She is very sympathetic, and I managed to speak to her alone before she saw Doris. She referred us to a neurologist who carried out some tests and arranged for a brain scan. He told me it was Alzheimer's Disease, and suggested I get in touch with Social Services as I would need help to look after her in the future. The Parkinson's diagnosis came about 18 months later, after she'd had a fall. She saw the neurologist again, and he said it was probable she now had Parkinson's Disease and multi-infarct dementia as well as the Alzheimer's.

Apparently it's possible for all three to happen in the same person. She has some medication for the Parkinson's, but she still has some shakiness in her hands and her walking is very slow—she seems to shuffle rather than really step out as she used to. I feel so sorry for her, to have all this happen to her—it doesn't seem fair.

Have you received much help from the Social Services and the other agencies?
Yes. After I'd been to their local office, a social worker called at the house, took down all our details, and arranged for a home help to come twice a week to help with some of the housework. I thought my wife would mind another woman coming into our house, but she was very accepting, and took to the home help really well. Then the social worker arranged a day-centre for Doris to go to twice a week; she enjoyed that, but as she's got worse they can't really manage her there now, so she stays at home. The social worker also put me in touch with the local Alzheimer's Disease Society group. The people there have been really helpful, and I've found out a lot about the disease and how to cope. As Doris has gone downhill, I've got more help from the district nurse; she's helped me get the pads to help with the incontinence at night. She also helps me give Doris a bath once a week. She needs one more than that, but I can't get her in and out of the bath on my own now, so we have to settle for a good wash down. I asked for a shower to be fitted in the bathroom, so that when she is incontinent she can be properly cleaned—it wouldn't be nearly so difficult for me to give her a shower. Anyway, someone from the Social Services came to assess her and agreed with me. The shower would be fitted 'as soon as possible'—that was a year ago! It would make such a difference to have it. We were also offered help with laundry—we go through so many clothes and so much bedding because of the incontinence. But it was no use because it was only delivered once a week—I would have needed loads more sheets to get by. So we bought a new automatic washing machine and tumble drier—they're nearly worn out now! We were given some money by the Alzheimer's Disease Society towards the cost, which was a great help.

Do you get any relief now?
Yes, I'm lucky enough to have a carer from Crossroads[1] who comes to sit with my wife one evening a week for a few hours while I pop out. The carer used to work in a hospital, so I feel quite happy leaving Doris with her. My family are very helpful as well. My daughter lives nearby, and helps me with shopping, and will sit with Doris whenever she can. Our son is further away, but he comes to stay with his family whenever he can, and that gives me a rest. It's good to have other people in the house I can have a conversation with; I get so lonely sometimes when Doris and I are on our own. We weren't always chatting before, but now there's no response at all I realise how much I miss just ordinary conversation. I think that's why it's so important for me to get out regularly—for company and conversation.

Do you think a time will come when you will be unable to look after your wife at home?
No, not if my health holds out. I think I can cope with the physical side of things fairly well. The only times I doubt whether I can continue are when I've been up what seems like half the night with her. The next morning I feel exhausted, not really ready to face another day. But she's not so disturbed at nights now—it's just a matter of changing the wet pad and sheet on the bed once during the night. I do worry what would happen if I were taken ill or had to go into hospital. I suppose Doris would have to go into hospital herself, but I'd rather cross that bridge when I come to it. To be honest, if she went away I don't know what I would do; looking after Doris is the most important thing in life to me now, and I want to carry on as long as I possibly can. She was a good wife to me; this is my way of showing my appreciation of her.

A wife's lament

Your husband is a very young sufferer. How old was he when the problems began?
He was about 39 at the time, although it was about a year later

[1]See Appendix

before I knew something was wrong. Apparently, his work mates had been covering for him at work for a year or so. He would forget what he was meant to be doing, just leave the job and wander off. It was a complicated job installing telephone systems—lots of wires, cables and connections. But the first I knew about it was when the firm wrote to him, saying he should go and see a doctor and have some sick-leave. So off he went to our family doctor, who's always been really helpful, and back he came, signed off for three months as 'unfit for work'.

What did you think was wrong at that time?
Well, to be honest, there wasn't much I could put my finger on. He was a bit distracted, lost in his own thoughts. I'd heard what had happened at work and thought perhaps he was a bit depressed. Not that there was much to be unhappy about: our children were twelve and eight and doing really well; we had a nice home; we both had steady jobs and were comfortably off. We got on well together, though he was a bit quiet and not very good at sharing his feelings. I suppose even then, at the back of my mind, I wondered whether it was the start of dementia. You see his mother died with dementia when she was 44. Over the years Mike had talked a lot about his mother's illness, so although I never knew her, I knew it hit her at about the same age. It had had a big impact on Mike because she went into a mental institution when he was seven, and he never saw her again. He wasn't allowed to visit her. She died when he was ten.

When was it confirmed that your husband had dementia?
It wasn't long before I knew for certain. Our GP sent him to a neurologist who had his suspicions. He then referred us to a psychiatrist who told me what I already suspected. This was about six months after he stopped working, so everything happened very quickly. It meant I had to stop putting the thought of dementia out of my mind, and face up to this disease that has changed the whole course of our lives. Very soon the firm made Mike redundant. They were very good about it. Our GP wrote them a medical report saying Mike was unlikely ever to be fit for work again.

How did Mike take losing his job?
Amazingly well really. The firm wrote saying it was because of his 'recent problems' and his need for rest, and he seemed to accept this. He knew there was something wrong, but he seemed to put it down to a stroke (which was what his father had had) rather than dementia. It was really odd one day. There was a programme on TV about Alzheimer's Disease. I tried to turn it off in case it upset him, but he insisted on watching it. At the end he just said. 'So that's what Mum had'. He didn't relate it to himself at all, but I could see it all happening before my very eyes. I had to fight to hold back the tears.

How did you explain what was happening to the children?
They realised very quickly. I discussed it with them and they decided to treat him as normally as possible, just to carry on with family life as much as we could. But they didn't like being left alone with him; our daughter especially began to get quite frightened of him as things got worse. They've been really resilient considering that our life as a family has been disrupted so much. My mother has been a great help—she lives just around the corner. Being retired, she's able to help out with the children when I'm out at work.

You've kept your full-time job. How have you managed to cope with the different demands of a career, a growing family and a sick husband?
With difficulty is the short answer! My job is essential for us to make ends meet financially. Mike was the breadwinner and my wages used to go on 'extras'. Now it's all we can do to manage the basics. I work in a big department store and the work is really tiring, so I sometimes come home feeling irritable and weary, which doesn't help. I thought about giving up work, but there's no way we could manage, and I'm not sure if I could stay at home all day: it's so good to get away from it all. As I said, my mother has been great with the children, and really we've received quite a lot of help with Mike in one way or another.

What help have you received?
The main thing has been the day-centre—it's run by the

Alzheimer's Society. He used to go down there on his own most days. The community psychiatric nurse introduced him to the other people. He was a bit erratic, sometimes losing track of time, but he usually got there in the end. He thought it was a sort of club for people who'd had strokes, so it didn't upset him to go. He used to take extra sandwiches because his appetite was enormous; he'd have two huge lunches and still want more. He loved it there—especially in the summer. Mike was a real open-air person; he loved sports, and would play ball-games in the garden with some of the young helpers. Eventually he started getting lost on his way there so they began to send transport for him. I wanted him to have some activity during the day because he was always such a fit and active man. The day-centre has been great from that point of view. We're lucky to have one that will take people of Mike's age—most day-centres seem to be for old people. Elaine, the community psychiatric nurse, has been very helpful; as things have got worse, I've been able to talk things over with her.

In what ways have Mike's problems got worse?
Looking back, it's all been very quick. Two years ago, when the diagnosis was first made, I could leave him at home all day with a list of jobs and he would do most of them. Then he started getting more distractable; lots of things would be left half-done; it would be obvious he'd had difficulty following the list of instructions I always left for him. Then I discovered that he was buying extra things at the supermarket and eating them before he got back. His appetite for food was incredible, quite uncontrollable—I couldn't reason with him about it. At first he was still driving, but the GP said we should stop him. I knew it might be dangerous, but I couldn't bring myself to tell him. Eventually, I got the GP to tell him he shouldn't drive in his condition, and we sold the car. Things gradually got worse; he started rummaging through bins, looking for things to eat; he even ate some bread off a neighbour's bird-table! I was so embarrassed, though the neighbours have always been really sympathetic and understanding. He began to get more unpredictable at home—perhaps it was because I was so tired and run-down. Anyway, he started to get violent, which was something so out of character. It was really frightening

because he's a big, strong man. I just cried and cried when he hit me, not just because I was hurt, physically and emotionally, but because I knew it was the end of the road. You see, the posibility of Mike going away had been raised before, by the CPN and our GP, but I'd always refused—even to give me a short break—because I knew Mike didn't want to go away. But when he hit me I knew there was no choice, and so now he's in a long-stay hospital. They've sedated him to reduce his aggression, and he seems reasonably settled now. We visit as often as we can. We've been told he'll probably not live for more than a few years, and I want to do my best for him. He was a good husband to me, and I don't want to let him down now. Sometimes when I've visited with the children, we all have a good cry when we get home. We try and remember what he was like before all this. He loves to see the children, though we're not sure he really recognises us all the time. We talk a lot about the old dad, when they were younger; we have to hold onto that. I just hope that they find a cure for Alzheimer's before our children are old enough to run the risk of having it. I would hate either of them to suffer what Mike has been through.

Many carers talk of having strong feelings of guilt, especially when it comes to having the sufferer placed in long-term care. Has this been your experience?
Yes, very much so. I know I've always done my best for Mike, but I can't help feeling that perhaps I've let him down. The worst time was when I had to start sleeping separately from him—his appetite for sex increased too. I just couldn't cope with it—I was so tired anyway—so I started to sleep in our daughter's bedroom. Then when I heard he was making sexual advances to the young female helpers at the day-centre, I felt so guilty, as if the whole thing was all my fault. But because of the way he had changed, I just couldn't bring myself to continue with the sexual side of our marriage. Later I felt really guilty when he went into hospital because I knew he didn't want that. Luckily, it's not the same hospital as the one his mother died in. That would have been awful for him. I just have to live with the guilt. I keep telling myself that I've done the right thing, and everybody has been really supportive, but it's a really

difficult feeling to shake off. I know I would have collapsed
with exhaustion if things had carried on as they were, and I had
to keep OK for the sake of the children, but I just wish it hadn't
come to that. If only we could have the husband and father we
remember so fondly back with us again...

Chapter Three

The impact of AD on the carer

Just as each AD sufferer is unique, with an individual pattern of disabilities and problems, so each carer's reaction to the problem is different. Each brings her own personality, experience, and ways of dealing with life's difficulties to bear, and each will have had her own unique relationship with the sufferer. In this chapter we consider some of the most common themes, the ones that crop up again and again, and the emotions and feelings—so often stressful and destructive—that tend to accompany them.

Grief

The title of this book likens the experience of being a carer for an AD sufferer to a bereavement—the person the AD sufferer used to be is no longer accessible or apparent, although still bodily present. Loss is inevitably a major feature of life for the carer, who may experience some or all of the following:
— loss of a companion and friend
— loss of someone with whom to share worries, concerns and joys
— loss of hopes and plans for a future together
— loss of social life
— loss of financial security
— loss of a job
— loss of interests and activities
— loss of a sexual partner
— loss of a source of support and comfort
— loss of a parent figure

— loss of recognition, when the person does not even know who you are
— loss of communication, when the person is unable to understand or make themselves understood
— loss of freedom, to be yourself

With any loss, it is well known that there is a process of adjustment, leading eventually to the person coming to terms with their loss—not forgetting it by any means, but being able to pick up the pieces of life once again. When the loss is sudden, there is often a period of shock, disbelief—it hasn't really happened, it can't be true, I'll wake up and find that everything is back to normal . . . These feelings may be particularly to the fore at the point when a diagnosis is made. Later, when the implications of what the doctor has said begin to sink in, the severity and inevitability of the progression of the disorder begin to be realised. But there is still a glimmer of optimism—surely they will get better; this can't be permanent, can it?

When we lose an object we start to search for it, looking everywhere—even in places where we know it cannot possibly be. When a loved one dies, the bereaved person begins the restless search for signs of life—amongst photographs, memories, anywhere . . . In a similar way, the person caring for an AD sufferer tries—wants—to find the person who is lost through all the confusion and perplexity. Couldn't the doctor be wrong? This can't *really* be AD. Perhaps tomorrow the mists of confusion will have cleared . . . And the AD sufferer's moments of lucidity further encourage this yearning, for just when you're getting used to the fact he has gone, there is this powerful reminder of the person you once knew.

In a bereavement the central feature is, naturally enough, sadness, distress, anguish and unhappiness. Other features, such as guilt and anger, can occur in the course of grieving—these will be discussed in more detail later. Many carers have times of extreme distress and unhappiness too; but the person getting over the death of a loved one has the mourning rituals to help him: the funeral itself; the friends who rally round and show sympathy; the fact that less demands are made on the person. The carer, on the other hand, continues to contend with the daily round of problems. Additional stresses crop up each day, making it even harder to adjust and get to grips with the strength of one's feelings. A supportive family helps in the case of a bereavement; but who can the carer confide in if it was the sufferer himself to whom she would normally turn? How can you adjust to something that is constantly changing and evolving? It is rather like aiming at a moving target; the adjustment has to be continuous whilst the caring goes on. There are many aspects of loss involved in caring for an AD sufferer; but the normal process of grieving is complicated by the continuing needs—for attention and care—of the sufferer himself.

Anger and resentment

There is more than enough to be angry about. All this loss ... Why should I suffer so much? Why me? Why should all those opportunities, all those things I cherished and longed for, be taken away from me? Why is so little help available? Why is the doctor/nurse/social worker so offhand with me? Why does no one listen? Why does my brother not help me more? How did I get trapped into this situation? Yes, there are many, many aspects of this disease and its effects that can make you angry and resentful even before we consider some of the things the sufferer may do which would try the patience of a saint.

When the person repeats the same question over and over again; when they wake you up for the third time during the night; when they refuse to get on the day-centre transport; when they turn away the helper you've spent hours arranging, saying they've got you to help them, why should they need anyone else!; when they follow you around the house, always under your feet, even calling you and knocking on the door when you're in the toilet; when they spit out the medicine that's meant to calm them down; when they misunderstand your help as a threat and lash out at you with their fist; when they get undressed five minutes after you've got them ready to go to the day-centre; when they wet their clothes just after you've taken them to the toilet with no result; when they're incontinent and faeces get everywhere; when ...

Yes, there can be many frustrations, irritations, hassles and aggravations. Each one on its own might be bearable once in a while, but they come thick and fast, and they are all a reminder of the continuing process of AD.

One of the problems with anger is that many of us are frightened to express it. Some of us have an in-built idea that anger is WRONG, particularly in a situation where the person is ILL. And so we pretend to ourselves that we're not really angry; we hold it in, keeping it under wraps deep inside. Unfortunately, it never goes away. It simply ticks away like a time-bomb, bringing bitterness and resentment in its wake. And when it finally explodes, it really is something to be frightened of. The explosion can be so powerful that, quite uncharacteristically, we turn on the AD sufferer, lose our temper, even shake them or slap their face or push them or . . .

There is no doubt that a point is often reached where the carer loses control altogether—and, it may be reassuring to know that when a carer is able to admit to others that this has happened, they, far from being shocked, begin to recount how the same thing has happened to them. No one is proud to have been in this situation, of course; many carers express great shame at what they have done and thought—but who can truthfully say they would not do the same in similar circumstances? In my experience, most situations where an AD patient suffers physical or verbal abuse arise from the enormous strain under which carers are placed and rarely from cruel, heartless relatives who have no feelings for the AD patient. Incidentally, I have come across many more instances of the patient being physically or verbally abusive to the carer than vice versa.

We must, however, learn from the experience of carers who have found themselves in situations that are intolerable for both parties. What can be done?

1   Recognise feelings of anger and irritation before they build up too much. Find someone you can talk to; get things off your chest; don't bottle up your feelings. Keeping them to yourself can actually do damage to your emotional and physical health—it is not really being virtuous to fool yourself and others into believing that you are calmness personified when in reality your emotions are seething below the surface.

2   Have escape routes planned. Can you go out for a walk when your blood is boiling? Or is there someone who would come round when needed to let you simmer down?

3   Remember, it is not the person you love and care for who is making you angry and resentful—it is this wretched disease, the uncalled for, unwanted intruder who is threatening to blight your life. It is the disease itself that merits your anger and frustration and rarely the patient.

4   When you feel you are losing control, you need extra help. Don't try to soldier on alone. Asking for help isn't an admission of failure. It's a realistic appraisal of a difficult, stressful situation. And make sure the situation *does* change so that you can remain in control of your feelings and not reach bursting point again.

Guilt

When a crisis or a worrying situation occurs, it is natural to seek out a cause, a reason, some explanation for what has happened. This search for a reason can lead to cases of AD being apparently 'caused' by a house move, a holiday, a bang on the head, retirement or a bereavement. Some of us go further than this and blame ourselves for what has happened. Perhaps there was something we did—or something we failed to do—that has led to this. If only I hadn't insisted on moving here; if only I had taken more notice of his worries about his memory; if only I hadn't been so busy; if only I'd taken her to the hospital sooner...

It seems to be part of some people's make-up to take the blame for all that happens around them and to find fault with their own actions and motives. Even if we can accept that the onset of AD is not our fault, the caring can be so difficult that it may be easy to find things we feel we should have done better, things we wish we hadn't said, or things that we couldn't manage to do. Part of the problem is that many people expect too much of themselves (the perfectionist is a good example of this). When we fail to achieve the impossible we then chastise ourselves as if we are abject failures. In the caring situation this may emerge when we have to share the care—allowing the person with AD to go into a home, a hospital or even a day-centre to give us a break. We feel guilty, saying to ourselves that any reasonable loving wife/husband/daughter/son/relative would be able to cope without such help; I am therefore a failure because I need help. What if the hospital finds the problems less severe? Does that mean that I haven't been looking after the person properly?

Feeling guilty about not being able to cope or remain calm and even-tempered at all times; about having negative feelings like embarrassment or even disgust at a person's behaviour, are very common emotions. Many of us find it hard to accept that we are not saints, nor always able to live up to the expectations of ourselves and others. It may be that the sufferer has a long-standing ability to instil guilt feelings in you. This may be the case with some parent-child relationships, especially if the child has been told time and time again that they do not match up to the parent's expectations.

Carers are human beings in difficult, stressful situations; negative emotions are not suprising—and guilt is amongst the most powerful. It is very important to become aware of these feelings and work towards a realistic appraisal of the situation, your abilities, and what you can realistically expect from yourself. You do the AD sufferer no favours if you try to do more than you are able to; if you try to press on alone when you need help, if you try to carry on when you're exhausted, stretched to your limit. Guilt can drive us on, desperately trying to make up for our failings; it is not a good basis for carer or sufferer.

Role reversal

A carer may find herself having to take on new tasks and responsibilities. A husband who has never been involved in domestic affairs, for example, may find himself doing the cooking, the cleaning and the laundry; a carer whose partner has always maintained the house and paid the bills may have to take over these duties as well. Assuming these new roles can be difficult enough, but when it comes to providing intimate physical care—taking the person to the toilet, washing, bathing and feeding—a whole new area of responsibilities opens up. Many carers will have done such things for their own children; but caring for your husband/wife/mother/father in this way is something rather different. Never before have they been so dependent on you; and in the case of a parent, there seems to be a complete reversal of roles. You are giving total care to a person who once provided for all your needs. Now the onus is on you to be the carer, and all your feelings for that person—fear, admiration, resentment, jealousy, satisfaction and love—are brought into play as you assume this new role for someone who was such a powerful formative influence on your life. Your parent, may not take readily to the dependent role, of course; it may fit them as uncomfortably as the role of carer fits you.

It's often said that as we grow into adulthood our relationship with our parents changes—from parent/child to one equality as adults. For many of us, however vestiges of the parent-child relationship remain. A chance remark, a particular tone of voice, the look on a face—all these things can take us back over the years and make us feel six or seven again, a naughty child, or a child longing for parental approval and recognition. Some of us remain more child-like than others, and more dependent on them for support, encouragement and approval into our adult years. Despite your parent's present condition of dependency, that ability to place you in a child-like position may still be retained, which of course makes it all the more difficult to provide physical care, take control of a situation, be a 'parent' to your own parent.

It is important to be aware of this influence on your feelings. Becoming a 'parent' in your right may be difficult, and it may be resisted by the sufferer who wishes to retain control. Many complex interactions and feelings will be at work, making it all the more important to take decisions dispassionately and be clear about the feelings that lead you one way or another. It is one thing to choose to look after your mother at home because she was so good to you as a child; but quite another when you cannot bear what she would say if you didn't carry on—perhaps accusing you of not being a loving child or even of letting her down. Your parent might not actually say or even be able to say these things—but you may well find yourself programmed to think them!

Embarrassment

One of the things that AD often brings about is a loss of social niceties. Even if the sufferer seems to retain an apparent social awareness (what the doctors call a 'well-preserved social facade'), the skills that are needed to maintain former relationships are often amongst the first to disappear. It is obvious that the factors governing our behaviour in different social situations are quite complex—there are things you can do or say in some situations that would give offence in others. Strong language may be acceptable at work, but not at a dinner party. The AD sufferer may lose the judgement necessary to match word and action to the subtle complexities of the situation. It may become embarrassing to continue to attend social functions where the implicit standards are higher than the sufferer can maintain.

As the disorder develops, the person may also begin to lose judgement in more familiar surroundings. One carer described how embarrassed her teenage daughter was when the carer's father emerged from the toilet with his trousers round his ankles in front of his granddaughter's friends. Going to friends or family for a meal becomes difficult when the sufferer's table manners become poor and eating becomes a messy business. Dealing with incontinence in somebody else's home is hard to carry off with aplomb—unless they are very good friends! How much impact this has on you and the sufferer depends on several factors:

1 How easily your friends are put off. Unfortunately, some people simply cannot cope with seeing someone else decline. They feel so aware of not knowing what to do or say that they stay away. Perhaps seeing the sufferer brings the problems too close to home and reminds them of the risk of such difficulties in old age. This is not helped by the belief—common amongst so many—that these problems are inevitable as one grows older—fear is a great impetus to embarrassment. Other friends are more able to deal with such problems and will understand the carer's need for continuing friendship and company.

2 How sensitive you are to what other people think. Some people are much more thick-skinned than others. They can behave with aplomb in situations where others would curl

up with embarrassment. One carer wrote a newspaper article describing how she and the AD sufferer had continued to eat out together. This was something they had always enjoyed. The article described how the carer, through a process of trial and error, had identified certain restaurants in London that were better suited to the needs of the AD sufferer. These were places that tended to be more tolerant, offering easy access, convenient toilet facilities, and staff who did not treat the sufferer's messy eating with disdain. This carer's persistence is admirable— how many of us would simply have given up after one bad experience! Developing a tougher attitude to 'what people might say' is essential if you and the sufferer are not to become prisoners in the home. For instance, if the sufferer needs assistance at the toilet, this becomes difficult if carer and sufferer are not of the same sex and only segregated facilities are available! One husband described how he would recruit the aid of a kindly looking female to check that the ladies toilets were empty; he would then assist his wife whilst his accomplice stood guard at the entrance! Ultimately, life and the enjoyment of life are much more valuable than the raised eyebrows of a few passers-by. Often the help of others—another carer or an understanding family member—can help you to face up to potentially embarrassing situations, and allow the continuation of shared pleasures and experiences.

3   How aware the sufferer is of their social failures. If the sufferer becomes upset in large social gatherings, there is little to be gained by insisting that he or she participates. It may be better to build on those situations where the person does feel more comfortable—in the company of a few familiar friends, for example, rather than with many new faces. If the person does become anxious and upset at a social gathering, try to work out what it is that the person found confusing, frightening or threatening, with a view to adapting the situation in the future.

A number of carers find that having to help the person with their intimate physical needs is rather embarrassing— particularly in the context of role reversal. Perhaps it would be helpful to consider the alternatives. Would it be better to get help with the particular task? Would a stranger be preferable? Some carers find it helpful to think of the person's body as something the person uses and not the actual person as such. It makes it all the more difficult, of course, if the sufferer too shows embarrassment at needing help in the bath, for example. Here it is vital to preserve the person's dignity by giving an acceptable explanation for your presence: 'I'm just here to make sure you don't slip as you get out of the bath,' for example; and to point out calmly that there's a job to be done which needs to be carried out smoothly and quickly for the benefit of both sufferer and carer.

Embarrassment can at times be reduced by forward planning. Neighbours and friends may stay away because of their own fears and uncertainties about how best to respond to the sufferer. Make sure that they are warned and informed about the problems, and told how to get the best out of the sufferer. Have simple reading material available about AD to lend out (see Appendix) so that their knowledge and understanding of the disorder and what you are experiencing is increased. Be ready to explain the effects of the disorder. One carer was very concerned because her mother screamed loudly at night, and she knew other people in the block of flats must be able to hear. Letting the neighbours know the reason for the screaming did not lessen the potential disturbance; but it did mean that the screaming would not be put down to more sinister causes. Having an explanation prepared can be useful in situations that could otherwise leave you speechless. For instance, one sufferer failed to recognise her husband one morning. She ran into the street, stopped a passing stranger and asked him to call the police to remove the intruder (her husband!) from her home. Having a prepared explanation might help in such circumstances: 'Have you heard of Alzheimer's Disease? That's right, it's a form of dementia where the person's memory goes haywire. My wife suffers from it, unfortunately. She's being seen regularly at the hospital. Sometimes she does things like this, I'm afraid.'

Sometimes the sufferer can seem very convincing, of course, —but the police are generally very sympathetic to such problems! As more and more is said and written about these disorders, there are fewer and fewer people with no knowledge of them, and increasingly people realise that they have known AD sufferers themselves. The more that carers are able to overcome their natural reticence and embarrassment, the more attention will be focused on AD as a serious condition that affects people in every locality.

Loneliness

Being a carer can be a lonely task. There is the loss of companionship with the sufferer and a loss of social life as a result of embarrassment or the sufferer's own disabilities. It may seem difficult—and even selfish—to leave the sufferer whilst you go out. Or you may simply lack the energy to meet new people, perhaps too tired and exhausted from your efforts. Or financial pressures may not allow you to continue with an active social life. Various people may call at the house, but so often they may be too busy to stop and chat once the purpose of their visit has been accomplished. Perhaps the loneliest time is in the small hours of the night—you've been awoken for the umpteenth time; the sufferer is fully dressed, ready to go to the shops; you feel exhausted, close to breaking point, and very, very alone.

Loneliness is a major risk for many carers; and it makes it even harder for them to cope with the problems. There is no simple solution, but it is well worth giving priority to maintaining friendships and social contacts. Not having anyone to talk to all day can be difficult enough; but having only conversations that are confused and full of crossed wires can lead to frustration and isolation. You must not allow caring for the sufferer to push everything else out of your life. This probably means sharing the care so that you have regular times to devote to your own needs, and it means planning ahead so that you have thought through in advance who you could ring in a crisis in the middle of the night. Sometimes it helps just to know that there is someone you could contact. Have the number of a 24-hour counselling service like the Samaritans (see Appendix) by your phone just in case you ever feel desperately alone in your plight.

For many of us, making new friends is an awesome task; not

everyone is naturally outgoing and gregarious. In general, we are more likely to make friendships when we meet others who have a shared interest or concern—this is why adult education classes, clubs based around particular activities or church groups are often recommended to people who feel lonely. Many carers find support and friendship at meetings and support groups for carers such as those organised by the Alzheimer's Disease Society. There you will find other people in your own situation, people who know and understand what you are going through.

Mixed feelings

It is of course very easy to concentrate on the difficulties of caring, but it must also be said that many carers experience positive feelings about their role. In a way it is this combination of positive and negative feelings that makes the task so demanding. If it's all positive, there's no problem; if it's all negative you have no qualms about leaving the situation. People for whom we feel deeply can so easily disappoint us, hurt our feelings, leave us wretched or seething with anger, make us feel trapped and controlled. The other side of the coin is that they also have a great capacity to make us feel loved and wanted, confident, strong, joyful and free. Love and hate are indeed often very close. They share an intensity of emotion, but they differ in direction. Think of the mixture of feelings that are present to some degree in any close relationship. In times of hardship and stress, the negative ones may come to the surface—but their presence shows how much you care for the sufferer, how important he or she is in your life. If you experience strong negative feelings, this does not necessarily mean you have changed. The fact is that your circumstances and your relationship with the sufferer have been turned upside down. New problems, new stresses have created an imbalance in your previous mix of feelings.

But what about the positive feelings? Although at times it may seem hard to envisage, a number of carers report feelings of warmth for the sufferer, and a sense of achievement in their caring task. One survey in the USA showed that some of the husbands caring for wives who had developed AD felt that their marriage had improved despite the illness. This demonstrates the amazing human potential for 'making the best of a bad job' or finding a silver lining in every cloud. It also reminds us that being a carer can be like having a full-time job. It can fulfil some of the functions of employment for the retired person or the one who has been made redundant. It provides meaningful, worthwhile activity, filling and giving structure to the person's day.

Many of the more positive feelings will be an extension of what has gone before. Warm, loving feelings may continue; a smile, a glance or an embrace may still have the same meaning. At times, the person may show gratitude for what you are doing. At other times, you may find yourself feeling sympathy, pity even, for the person's plight. For many there is a sense of satisfaction in being able to give something back to the person. In the past they may have been good to you; they may even have cared for you. Now you have an opportunity to give something back to them, to thank them in a tangible way, and to show your appreciation for past kindnesses. For others, it may be not so much a thank you that is being expressed as an apology. Some carers feel they are able to make recompense for their past failings as a son or daughter, husband or wife.

Some carers find moments of satisfaction in the caring task. One carer who had given up a job as a senior executive with an international company to look after his wife described his tremendous sense of achievement when he worked out how to use the incontinence garments that had been supplied for her. Another one described her pleasure when she managed to get through to her mother after a lot of hard work. She responded with a smile. Yet another described his feeling of contentment when the sufferer finally slept at night, looking so peaceful, warm and secure. A daughter described with joy how she had finally persuaded her mother to help out again in the kitchen, something she had done automatically before the onset of AD. For many people, setting targets, tasks to be accomplished, provides something to work towards, something to be achieved. In the case of AD this may mean taking only tiny steps forward, aiming at 'successes' that would have seemed trivial before AD struck. To set your sights too high is to court disappointment—hoping for a cure or a dramatic change is almost certain to be unrealistic. Where a large family gathering might once have given carer and sufferer much pleasure, now having a couple of people happily to tea may be what is feasible. The carer may once have been in charge of a large work-force; now he or she may have to settle for the equally demanding task of co-ordinating help in the home and visits to the day-centre, together with hospital appointments and calls by the family doctor. AD requires a different focus from most of the other situations of life; but for those who relish a challenge, there are small victories to be won, and carers can feel some pride in their achievements. AD always presents fresh challenges, of course; no one can ever feel they have really mastered it. As it fluctuates and progresses, new situations arise and new problems present themselves. One carer said, 'We used to wonder how we would manage in a year or two; now I'm happy to get through each day—that's more than enough to cope with.'

Some carers feel a sense of purpose when they consider the alternatives. Things may be difficult at home, but at least the sufferer is not in an old people's home—or the local psychiatric hospital, the very name of which may cause distress because of the stigma and fear attached to it over the years. That can prove a real source of satisfaction—the fact that the carer is managing to look after the person in his own home, keeping him out of a feared institution. Others are keeping a promise, to the sufferer or to a deceased relative, to 'look after mum' or never to let the person go into a home. Obviously, such commitments have to be felt very strongly if you are to maintain them when the going gets tough; but these are some of the ways in which carers do derive a sense of satisfaction of a worthwhile job being done, in a difficult, often demanding, situation.

The final source of mixed feelings arises when there is an apparent conflict of interest between sufferer and carer. The classic example is when you have decided you need a break and have arranged for the sufferer to receive care for a day, a week or whatever. When you take the sufferer to the place where they are to stay, they beg you not to leave them in there. Your emotions are torn; you know that you desperately need a rest because you're feeling exhausted; and yet how can you ignore the equally desperate plea of the person you care so much about? If you are strong-minded in your resolve you will inevitably feel twinges of guilt and concern during your period of relief. These emotions will conflict with the other feelings of peace and freedom—peace from noise and repeated questions, freedom from being on call all the time, from having constant demands made upon you. Such a conflict of feelings often prevents carers taking up sorely needed offers of relief care. It can be argued that it is actually in the best interests of the sufferer for the carer to have rest when required; if the carer doesn't have relief, he or she may soon reach a point where they cannot carry on at all. 'Take care of yourself' is perhaps a good motto for any carer. Such a resolve will, however, require finding ways around some of the conflicts of interest that are bound to occur. Moral support from friends, family and concerned professionals can be a great help in such circumstances.

The stages of caring

There is no definite, ordered sequence of feelings through which all carers inevitably pass. So much depends on the particular circumstances of the relationship between the sufferer and carer. It is possible however to identify some themes that may come to the fore at different periods of time.

At first, the main thought could well be, 'What's happening? What's going on?' Both sufferer and the carer-to-be may share puzzlement at sudden lapses or subtle changes. Although at this point the changes may be quite inexplicable, it is only natural to seek out a reason for what is happening. Sometimes the sufferer is blamed—they are said to be difficult, awkward or lazy. Sometimes it is assumed that the sufferer is worried about something in particular—retirement perhaps, or difficulties at work or in the family. Sometimes the problems seem to coincide with a health problem, an accident, a house move or even a holiday, and so the blame is placed on some recent event. Sometimes the fault is thought to lie with the relationship itself—the sufferer's withdrawal may lead to relatives feeling hurt and rejected, as well as perhaps burdened by the extra responsibilities that begin to be transferred from sufferer to carer. It may help a little if the sufferer is able to talk to you about their problems. Usually though it seems that the person is either not aware of the difficulties or is unable to admit to them.

Finding a reason for the changes is important, but settling on the wrong one can have unfortunate consequences—such as blaming the sufferer for something that he or she cannot control. This is why it is important for an accurate diagnosis to be made. Sometimes the first attempt to obtain medical opinion does not lead directly to an accurate diagnosis. Carers report, for example, that the problems are dismissed by some doctors as merely symptoms of old age; or perhaps the results of the diagnostic assessments are puzzling to the professionals concerned. There can then follow a period of uncertainty and even disappointment—having taken the step of seeking professional advice, you are no closer to understanding the problem. If the problems are not taken seriously, the carer may well feel angry, especially when it has taken a lot of heart-searching, effort and persuasion to bring the sufferer to the attention of the professional services.

Sooner or later, the day comes when you know 'officially' what you may always have feared and even hardly dared to consider. For some the moment comes at a hospital; for others at a doctor's surgery or even at home after a professional's visit. Sometimes, the realisation comes from an accumulation of comments and advice, never clearly spelt out. Of course, even when the facts are clearly presented to you, it is quite probable they will not sink in immediately. Some carers find themselves in a state of shock and disbelief at this point. Even though you were prepared for the news, the apparent finality of the diagnosis can be hard to absorb. If it comes out of the blue, you may feel dazed for some time. Again, it is natural to wonder, to hope, that some mistake may have been made, even if you knew in your heart all along what the hospital would say. Gradually the acceptance grows that you are faced with a basically incurable, progressive condition. This is the time to find out all you can so that you know what you are dealing with. It is the time to go back to the hospital and ask all the questions you couldn't ask at the time because the news had yet to sink in. It is the time to read, and to discover there are other carers in your position. Some of what you hear may worry you greatly—the description of the effects of very severe dementia, for example. In a sense, you can only cross that bridge if and when you come to it; it is worth remembering that such a severe state is not always inevitable. Knowing about it will mean that you are not taken unawares later on.

At each stage in the disorder there is much to be learned from the experiences and ideas of other carers, and such knowledge can help you to feel that you have some control over the progress of the disorder. At this point there may well be fears about the future. It is vital not to keep these fears to yourself. Talk them over with someone who can help you to put them in perspective and plan for the immediate future.

After the diagnosis has been made there could be a lot to do. The person's financial affairs will have to be dealt with—a process that in the UK can be quite complicated. The hospital may have suggested various forms of help you had not been receiving previously; arranging these can be quite a task. Now you know what is wrong you may be changing your approach to the sufferer (especially if you thought before that the person was simply becoming lazy!). You may be struggling to find ways of coping with some of the problems that prompted you to consult the professional services in the first place. This is the point at which you can, almost without knowing it, be sucked into the role of care provider. You must step back and look at your own situation, mobilise other sources of help—from family and the professional services—rather than allow a pattern to be established from which it could be hard to break free later.

After diagnosis the time scale of the different phases varies enormously from person to person. For some the struggle to cope with the person's need for care can go on for some time. For others, feelings of strain, exhaustion and depression surface more quickly. No one seems able to help; everything seems hopeless. Perhaps the carer's health is also beginning to suffer. The question arises of how long the carer can go on in this way. Often it is hard for the carer to accept more help in such a frame of mind. These feelings of overwhelming strain can be very frightening; some carers fear they are going mad or that they will lose control. It is vital to be aware of the strain and to find ways of reducing it before it reaches such levels.

This may mean accepting more help and relief, or facing up to your own limitations. How much can you really manage? At some point you might have to consider the possibility of the person going into a home or a hospital. Tremendous guilt may be brought on by such a move, particularly if you had promised yourself (or the sufferer) that you would never allow this to happen. Standards of care in hospitals and homes always lack the personal touch a carer can provide; conditions are often far from ideal. Finding a suitable place is often not easy. This can then be a very trying time. The person may be accepted at one home on a 'trial' basis. If found unacceptable, you have to start all over again. Even if it is only a temporary break that you are seeking, the same difficulties may apply, added to which you have the potential upset and disturbance for the sufferer in having to adapt to different places. Letting go can be very difficult. Your concerns for the sufferer may lead to your not benefiting as much as you need to do from the period of relief care. Either in person or in spirit you remain behind with the sufferer, rather than enjoying this opportunity to relax and be yourself—which was, after all, the whole point of the exercise.

Eventually, the day-to-day caring comes to an end; the sufferer is settled into long-term care or death releases the person from the downhill path. Now the task is to pick up the pieces of life again. You may find yourself feeling guilty because you are relieved that it is all over. Some, more positively, feel a sense of achievement—all that could be done *was* done. At this point the extent of how immersed you have become in the caring role becomes evident—suddenly there is a huge void.

Where the person is in long-term care, some carers choose to spend a fair bit of time at the home or hospital, helping with the care of the sufferer; others prefer to withdraw further at this stage. Where the hospital is a long way off the choice may be made for you. This is the time to make yourself aware of your own needs; to look for nurture and refreshment for yourself. Some carers literally collapse at this point—only nervous energy had kept them going this long. It can take time to find meaning in your life once more; to re-discover old relationships that have been neglected, or to develop new ones. Your need for emotional support will continue for some time. Some carers find it helpful to continue meeting with other carers for a while; some work in a voluntary capacity to help other carers. Others want a complete break. Being a carer can leave its mark upon you. Sometimes the wounds take a long time to heal.

Marriage and sexuality

If your spouse develops AD, your relationship will inevitably be altered in many ways. Common interests may be lost; a sense of partnership may seem a thing of the past; emotional support may have to be sought from other quarters. This is particularly hard if your spouse was the one with whom you would talk over any problems, the one in whom you confided your innermost thoughts and feelings. Much will depend of course on what the relationship was like before. To put it bluntly, if you didn't get along beforehand, caring for the sufferer will be much more difficult and tiresome. The extreme example of this is where the carer was actually contemplating separation and divorce before the condition developed. In this case, AD may be seen as trapping the person in an unwanted relationship, leading to much bitterness and resentment. On the other hand, where the marriage was warm and mutually satisfying, this will give a firm base from which to face up to the difficulties of caring—although the effects of AD on the sufferer will be equally, if not more, upsetting than if there had been no love lost between the couple.

Obviously, AD will bring about major changes in the marriage. Once upon a time each partner may have had their own tasks and areas of responsibility; now more and more will have to be taken on by the carer. This can be difficult if the sufferer is sufficiently aware to see the spouse taking over particular jobs, but is unable to understand why. For example, the sufferer may object to the spouse sorting out the finances or cooking the meals if he or she formerly fulfilled that role. The objections can sometimes be overcome by involving the sufferer as far as possible in the task so that he or she does not feel excluded. Of course, the nub of the problem is that these situations provide a tangible reminder to the sufferer of what is really happening to them, and few can cope with such an awful reality with good grace. Similarly, the tasks that have to be taken on may become a focus of concern for the carer too. They are a reminder of how much has changed, how much has been lost; in addition to which, the carer may feel that he or she lacks the skills required to carry them out adequately. Suddenly there may be a great deal to learn all at once, adding further to the problems of being a carer.

In some marriages, all may not have been perfect in the past. The carer may feel, however, that this was to a large degree the result of his own failings. In this instance those feelings of guilt, regret or remorse may be channelled positively into caring for someone who stood by you and did so much without being properly appreciated. Surveys have suggested that this is more likely to be a motivation for husbands, although this may not always be the case. In the case of wives, the fact that they have enjoyed a warm and loving relationship in marriage is one of the strongest factors in making the caring bearable.

There is no doubt that AD changes every aspect of the marriage. Communication is impaired; talking things through together may become impossible quite early on in the disorder, and feelings of warmth, affection, admiration and respect tend to be replaced by sympathy or pity. The changes are reflected also in the sexual area of the marriage. Here again, patterns established earlier on in the relationship will have an impact; as will, of course, the specific disease-related changes in the sufferer. Sometimes this can result in a continuation of the status quo—warmth and affection may continue to be shared physically and sensually; or sexual communication may remain an important aspect of the interaction between husband and wife. However, some situations which the spouse may find more difficult may arise. One such is where the carer's sexual desire continues but, for one of a variety of reasons, sex with the spouse is no longer possible. The sufferer may have lost interest (as in other areas of life); or perhaps the sufferer was the person who previously took the initiative and now no longer does. The sufferer may no longer be physically capable; or the couple may be separated for short-term relief or long-term care. There may be emotional reasons why a sexual relationship now seems impossible. If the sufferer no longer seems to be the person the carer married, how can physical intimacy continue? Or perhaps the deterioration in the sufferer's behaviour, habits and hygiene become obstacles to continuing physical affection. Another difficulty arises where, far from losing sexual drive, the sufferer's desire for sex increases or continues in such a way that the carer finds it unwelcome. Whatever the reason, the end result for the carer may well be frustration and lack of fulfilment. This is a further loss to bear, and this time in the presence of the strongest possible reminder of what once was—in the shape of the spouse's physical being.

There are no easy answers to these difficulties and no standard pattern of changes in this area. It is essential that carers for whom these issues loom large talk to someone who is at ease and comfortable with these matters. This is one area where it can be difficult to turn to family or friends, however supportive they may be in other respects. A professional counselling service is invaluable. The British Association for Counselling (see appendix) may be able to advise on where to find counselling locally. Sometimes it is actually easier to talk to a stranger about such personal matters, especially when you know that what you say will remain confidential.

It's a family problem

For many carers the most important help they receive is from other family members. In some families care is shared—two daughters may take it in turns to look after their mother for example. In others, a family member who lives some distance away from the sufferer and the main care-giver makes a regular commitment to have the person to stay for a couple of weeks at a time while the carer has a break. Even when practical help cannot be offered for one reason or another, another relative may be able to provide invaluable emotional support for the carer. One wife of an AD sufferer described how being able to telephone her daughter at times of stress and despair was a godsend. Even though her daughter was too busy with her own young family to provide any practical help, her offer of a sympathetic ear was just what the mother needed.

For other carers, one of their biggest sources of regret and distress is how little help other members of the family offer.

'My brother just doesn't want to know; he asks how mum is when he phones, but he never offers to take her.' 'My children don't seem to realise how difficult it is for me to look after their father. When I tell them some of the things he's done recently they look as if they don't really believe me.' Some carers feel alone, isolated from those they had expected to be of help. Others feel bitter and resentful—perhaps they have become the 'carer' by the fact that they were the only child remaining in the family home. They resent the assumption that they will be the one who takes responsibility for their parent, and perhaps feel envious of the brothers and sisters who have 'escaped', and seem now to be getting on with their lives without the burdens the carer is experiencing.

Families are where we experience some of our most intense emotions—joy and happiness, as well as anger, sadness and resentment. Families differ greatly from each other in a number of different ways: how close the members remain—geographically and emotionally; how much help they expect and offer at times of trouble; who is considered a 'close' or a 'distant' relative; as well as how well the various members communicate and get on with each other. Each family has its own way of dealing with problems. In some families everybody rallies round to help; in others it is left to one or two people to sort things out. In certain families, problems are never discussed openly; in others again, there are major divisions—A will talk to B, B will talk to C, but A will not enter the same room as C! Families do not remain static, of course; as powerful members are lost, new patterns become established; as family members form partnerships with members of other families, they may find themselves in two quite different, even conflicting, patterns of family life. As family members pass through the different phases of their lives, the degree to which their other responsibilities and interests pull them away will vary. Despite the various changes, the influence of the family 'rules' can still loom large. 'My mother looked after her mother for 20 years; I have to look after her now she needs help.' 'I promised my mother I'd look after Dad if anything happened to her, so I had to take him in.' 'Although she's actually my aunt, she looked after us when we were children, and eventually looked after my children while I was at work, so that's why I look after her now.' 'When we were kids, Dad was always coming home the worse for drink—I've got no time for him now.' Events in the past have a big impact on the AD sufferer's situation in the present.

Of course, it is often said that families no longer care as they did in the past or as they do in other cultures. The myth seems to be that old people in particular are not supported by their families as they would have been, say, in Victorian times. Have 'family rules' changed to that extent? Has the fabric of a caring society come apart at the seams? There are several issues worth considering in this respect. First, the proportion of older people has increased considerably so that families would need to care MORE to maintain previous standards. Secondly, families are now smaller on average, so there is less opportunity for care to be shared amongst the different members. Thirdly, historians remind us that in the UK, Victorian society was not altogether caring and compassionate. Many people with dementia would have been committed to the much feared workhouse. Conditions were harsh and inmates were not treated by and large with dignity or respect. Similarly, in other cultures that are sometimes held up as examples of family care, the proportion of old people is much smaller. In countries where the proportion of old people is rising there are already reports of care rapidly breaking down—even of old people being abandoned on the streets. Where it is socially unacceptable to ask for help, families may resort to such extreme solutions in sheer desperation. Don't believe all the myths you hear about family care in the past or in other countries.

An area where particular problems may arise is where a married child is looking after a parent. Inevitably, the caring that the son or daughter undertakes will have an impact on the spouse and their children. Sometimes the carer will be fully supported by his or her spouse—it is sometimes pointed out that daughters-in-law in particular often take on a great deal of the day-to-day responsibility for caring. At other times, the caring can cause friction between husband and wife, with one partner perhaps resenting the amount of time that is being devoted to mother- or father-in-law at the expense of their own 'family'. The amount of time devoted to one's respective families is an important issue for any married couple. The increasing demands of AD may well threaten to upset the previously established pattern, and there is then a need for a new arrangement to be agreed between the couple. Some couples are better at adapting to changing circumstances than others. If both partners are not in agreement, tension, friction and resentment are likely to occur. Relationships with in-laws are not always smooth at the best of times; you can choose your partner, but his or her family are not necessarily seen as part of the marital contract! If your partner has never got on with your parents—they may have disapproved of your choice or simply never seen eye-to-eye with him or her—AD is hardly going to make things better. There may come a point where you feel that you are being pulled between your love for your parent and your love for your partner. Sometimes this is even expressed as an ultimatum: you are to choose between your parent and your partner. Unfortunately, when such situations occur they are not readily resolved. Even if you decide to place your parent in a home, your marriage may well not recover instantly. After all, there has been a breakdown of communication and support between you; it may be hard to forgive and forget when you are still getting over the trauma of your parent going into a home. Getting the marriage right again could well take a lot of work, and you may need outside help for this—from a marriage guidance counsellor, for example. The best way to prevent these problems building up is by agreeing with your partner the limit of your involvement; discussing each step; sharing your reasons for wanting to provide care; listening to your partner's concerns; and working together to try to overcome the problems you will face. This can never be more important than when you are contemplating bringing your parent into your own home. If you and your partner are not fully of one mind on this you would be well advised not to pursue it further. The effect can be so devastating on your marriage and family life that only a couple who are equally committed to this step have any hope of making it work. Preserving time for each other and your own children, space and privacy, entertaining at home—so many areas of life are potentially changed when an AD sufferer moves into your home that it has to be thoroughly thought through and agreed by all concerned.

When AD hits a person younger in life, the effects on family life are especially tragic. This is the time of life when the person may be fulfilling the role of parent to a growing family and providing a substantial, if not the major, contribution to the family's finances. A home is still being developed and established, there are many plans and hopes for the future. Now the carer has to cope as if he or she were a single parent, with all the financial and parenting problems that entails. There is also the AD sufferer himself to be cared for, a person struck down in the prime of life when the future seemed so full of promise and potential. It will be difficult for the carer to continue working, but if the job is given up the financial problems will be worse and the future prospects for the family even less secure. Before deciding to give up work, the carer will have to consider how easy it would be to re-enter the job market in a few years' time. This is a situation where you will need all the help you can get, both practical and emotional, to deal with the trauma of what is happening to your family.

A matter of especial importance will be the effects on the children. What should they be told? Will they be safe with the sufferer? Should the children's friends come to the house? How do I give the children the time they need when my spouse needs so much help? Much will depend on the ages of the children, of course. Younger children may accept that Mum or Dad is not well; it will be important to ensure that the child understands that what is happening is not the child's fault. Older children and teenagers will be able to understand more of the details of the parent's disorder. Each child will probably need opportunities to talk over what is happening with someone outside the family; it may be very difficult for the carer alone to give the children as much emotional support as they will need. Some older children may find it difficult to talk openly about the problems with you—perhaps not wanting to upset you by disclosing their own feelings of embarrassment or resentment. Again, an outside person can help; and it is well worth making sure that the children's schools know about the problems. Whatever the age of the children, do what you can to encourage them to spend time with the sufferer, building up memories of enjoyable moments together. Try to find things the sufferer can enjoy doing with the child—playing card games, watching TV; playing with bricks if it is a younger child, for example. The sufferer may really enjoy the affectionate demonstrativeness of a young child sitting on his or her lap, giving cuddles and so on. Teenagers may be able to help you think of ways of tackling some of the problems that arise, and may be recruited into giving practical help. It will of course be harder emotionally for children who are old enough to have known the parent well before AD developed; they will have to cope with the loss of a parent they once knew. Younger children can be much more accepting of the person they find now. As far as possible, openness should be encouraged and the children's friends welcomed. Explanations may be needed, and care taken to make sure a father with AD does not emerge from the bathroom with no trousers on when teenage girls are around. The alternative is to keep the problems hidden and secret, which will really not help your family to give the support and understanding you deserve. With teenagers generally, it is wise to be subtle with your encouragement so that they do not feel pushed into doing something or another. Be open with them, clear in your requests; allow them choices and opportunities to take responsibility. Do not look to them for your own emotional support—that must come from outside the situation. Thus, while it is good to share your feelings with them, it is important to beware of draining their resources to meet your own needs. Plan regular times when your children can have your full attention—it is worth getting extra help if this is otherwise impossible. Unless there are special difficulties there should not be any problem regarding safety—although the AD sufferer's lack of judgement makes them a poor choice as a babysitter! With young children, you will want to make sure someone else is around.

Similar issues can be raised in relation to the involvement of grandchildren with an older AD sufferer. If the contact is carefully structured and monitored, both parties can benefit greatly. Sometimes grandchildren seem to have more patience and creativity in their dealings with the sufferer than their parents! Perhaps their slightly more distant relationship helps them to be less emotionally involved than someone who is experiencing the gradual loss of a parent.

When the carer is the only child of an AD parent, particular pressures may be brought to bear. The possibilities for sharing the care are obviously reduced; the expectation that he or she will provide whatever care is needed whatever their present life circumstances may seem overwhelming. Often an only child's relationship with the parent is somewhat more intense, undiluted by the presence of other children. This can make it harder for him or her to step back and view the situation dispassionately.

It is important to mobilise whatever family resources are available. If one person has already become the main carer he or she will need to take the initiative—the rest of the family may be only too happy to let the carer continue! How can you get the family to pull together? One way is to call a family meeting to discuss the care of the sufferer. Make sure everyone is informed about the condition—give them some of the booklets that are available about AD and other dementias (see appendix). Make clear at the meeting what you are already doing for the sufferer; one powerful method is to keep a diary of all that you have done for the sufferer over the previous week, including the difficulties you have faced. Explain clearly and precisely what help you would find useful, and the limits of your own involvement. You may say, for example: 'Some alternative care is needed for mum whilst we go on holiday in June and October.' Or: 'Our house is too small for us to take dad to live with us, but I can visit him 4 or 5 times a week.'

The aim is to get everyone working together, each contributing what he or she has to offer without any particular family member feeling trapped or overwhelmed by the caring. Sometimes less tangible support can be helpful in itself—knowing that other family members appreciate what you are doing and are prepared for you to unburden yourself to them from time to time. If there are tensions and conflicts in the family, it would be worth considering enlisting the help of a social worker or other professional to act as 'referee' for the meeting, thus ensuring that it focuses on the problems at hand, that everyone has a chance to be heard, and to maintain a constructive atmosphere when the different possibilities for the care of the AD sufferer are being freely discussed.

Finding ways of coping

At some point you will need some freedom from the daily routine and the demands of caring in order to take a step back and look at what you are doing, even to consider the feelings you are experiencing. A friend or another family member could help with this perhaps. It may help to discuss your situation with a friend or a counsellor—not for them to provide solutions, but for you to have a sounding-board for your own ideas and concerns.

Use this time to take stock of yourself and your situation. Ask yourself why you are caring for this particular person. Are those reasons strong enough, given the changes that being a carer will make/are making to your own life? Ask yourself what resources you have. Good health? Patience? Strength of mind? Unflappability? Do you have a caring partner? Good friends? A supportive family? Are there good health and social services in your area should you need them? Ask yourself about the sufferer too. Did you previously have a good relationship with him or her? Does the sufferer tend to be fairly co-operative and undemanding? If the answers to any of these questions is no, it doesn't mean that you should not continue as a carer, but you need to be aware of the potential difficulties ahead.

Try to work out what your own needs are at this phase in your life—work, family, marriage, social life and so on. It is tempting to see caring as a temporary phase during which you forget your own needs and make them subservient to the needs of the sufferer. The problem here is that this 'temporary' phase has an unspecified length, at the end of which you may have lost some sense of yourself—your own needs, your own identity even. Ideally, the aim would be to find ways of meeting both the sufferer's needs and your own. You need to strike a balance, preserving time and energy for your own interests, health, friends, social life and other occupations. It is not selfish to think in this way. It is in the best interests of the sufferer to have carers who are relatively relaxed and at ease, with an interest in life and outside contacts—all of which enrich the caring relationship.

Let us then summarise some of the ways of coping with the problems of caring:

1   Find and ask for the support you need—both practical and emotional—from family and friends and the various service agencies. Other carers may be the best people to suggest the most useful sources of help outside your immediate circle; they can be met through the various carers' organisations.

2   Prevent anxiety and depression taking hold by finding ways to relax and unwind—yoga, breathing exercises, relaxation exercises, music and walking, for example. Try to establish more control over what is happening—you can't make AD go away, but there are practical steps that can be taken to make some of the problems less difficult (see Chapter 4). Identify the positive reasons you have for being a carer, the ways in which you are actually succeeding in the midst of a tremendously difficult situation.

3   Deal with your negative feelings. Don't bottle them up. This is harmful for all concerned. Choose safe release mechanisms so that you won't have further regrets later. Talk your feelings through with someone you trust or find ways to let off steam—by physical exercise, for example, thumping a pillow, or screaming in a secluded spot! Learn to spot when your anger is getting out of control and find ways of defusing the situation—by leaving the room for a few minutes, counting to ten, or reciting a favourite poem.

4   Make sure you have regular times to yourself, making use of day-care or longer periods of relief from time to time. Use the time for your own needs; fill it in such a way that you cannot spend it thinking and worrying about the sufferer.

5   Get all the help you can. Don't feel you're not entitled to it or that it's an admission of failure. The sufferer needs to become used at an early stage to the caring being shared by several people so that it's not assumed later on that you will do everything. When a new problem comes along, think what extra help you need to deal with it, don't assume immediately that you must do it yourself. Co-ordinating lots of different helpers sometimes seems more trouble than it's worth, but in the long run it's the best way of ensuring you don't become trapped and isolated in a situation with which you cannot cope.

6   Look after yourself! Keep your sense of identity. Recognise the importance of your own needs.

Chapter Four

Coping with the problems of AD—some general principles

In the previous chapter we discussed some ways in which carers can reduce their level of stress and combat the onset of depression and despair. These matters are of vital importance if the carer is to cope with all the problems that can accompany AD. In this chapter we describe a general approach to the AD patient that can help keep problems to a minimum and provide guide-lines for assessing the various situations that may arise. In later chapters some of the more common problems are discussed, together with some ways of tackling them. These proposed strategies are based on certain approaches that other carers have found helpful. Part of coping successfully is sharing the care, so we will also consider making choices about places where the sufferer can be cared for, either for a short break, or in the longer-term. The general aim is not to prescribe how care should or should not be given—such generalisations are bound to break down given the range of problems and disabilities—but to increase the information and choices available to carers so that they can make the decisions best suited to the needs of the individual situation.

Be adaptable

For most people coping with AD is a completely new experience. Sometimes people compare it with looking after a child, but there are in fact many differences because of the person's previous experience of being an adult. In view of its impact on the person's memory and patterns of thinking, it is quite different from providing care for any other disability. What is more, no two patients are the same. The consequence is that every approach must be unique, developed with experience over time. On top of this, the disorder fluctuates and progresses; what is successful one day may not be at all useful the day after; what works early on may become irrelevant as the disabilities worsen. Flexibility is the order of the day. There's no point in changing things for the sake of change, of course—by all means stick to the things you do find helpful—but when they no longer help, alternatives must be sought. If at first you don't succeed—try another way! You may be surprised to discover just how many different approaches are possible. If you ask different people how they, say, encourage the person to have a wash, you'll find as many ways as there are carers! Hopefully, the specific ideas given in later chapters will help you to create your own strategies. The first step in any problem-solving is to identify exactly what the problem is; it's always worth asking, 'Does it have to be a problem?' In other words, some problems can be avoided or got round rather than actually solved. If the person won't have a bath, for example, but *will* have a good all-over wash, is it worth making a fuss over the bath? If the person will use a spoon to eat, but not a knife and fork, could this not be accepted? To adapt to and accept the changing circumstances is important. Some things are difficult to accept, and this is where the main efforts should be directed—at changing the things that really matter.

Striking a balance

Sometimes people ask how much they ought to encourage the sufferer to do things for herself. Surely they argue, it's good to stimulate her mind, exercise her brain, or she'll get even worse, won't she? Others say, 'When we try to persuade mother to do things, she just gets upset'. We are up against two polar opposites here; and therefore we need to find a middle way. If the carer does too much for the patient, there is a risk that what skills remain will disappear more quickly. On the other hand, if the person is left to do everything for himself, he will of course fail and probably become distressed. It is certainly possible to put the person under too much pressure and give them too little support. It is also possible to make the person more dependent, less capable than they need be, and in so doing deny them opportunities to show a degree of independence. The middle way involves giving the person enough support and help for them not to be exposed to failure and undue stress, but sufficient stimulation and demand so that they have the opportunity to use their remaining skills and be as independent as is possible. Again, the fact that the illness varies so much from person to person makes this balance harder to achieve than with other disabilities where the person's skills may remain more or less constant from day to day. It means standing back, allowing the person to try, and only intervening as gently and tactfully as possible if and when it becomes clear that today the person is not able to complete that particular task. Even then, it can be possible to intervene in such a way as to help the person to continue, rather than take over from them totally. It means saying 'let me help you with that', rather than, 'here, let me do it for you'. Giving just enough help to get the person started again, or breaking up the task into smaller, more manageable chunks, helps to keep the person involved. She may not be able to go to the kitchen and make a pot of tea, but with supervision she can perhaps get the cups out, put the tea bags in the tea-pot and so on. Talking the person through a task can sometimes compensate for the difficulty of remembering the sequence of actions. The sufferer may be able to exercise choice if alternatives are presented clearly enough. A choice between two dresses may be possible; but if you had asked, 'what would you like to wear today?' you may not have received an answer. At most, three options should be offered, and if possible they should be shown to the person to avoid making further demands on memory. It can be so much easier to decide *for* the sufferer; but always to do so makes it even more difficult for the person to feel any semblance of control over his or her life.

The advantages of this balanced approach are that you keep the person's loss of skill to a minimum; in addition to which, they retain their dignity and self-esteem and avoid feeling completely helpless and hopeless for as long as possible. The consequence is that they don't avoid situations unnecessarily for fear of failing. Fear of failure can so often lead to apparent loss of interest and skill. By helping the person to avoid it, he is much more likely to continue to participate in activities and events that interest him. Striving to maintain this balance takes time; it takes longer to encourage someone to dress himself or feed himself; it can be so much quicker to do it for him than give him just enough support, help and encouragement to do it for himself. In the longer term, however, you may be saving yourself time by helping to retain the person's skills and, just as important, some remnants of dignity and self-respect.

Maintaining communication

There are many barriers to effective communiction with an AD sufferer. Keeping the channels of communication open, however, is vital if further frustrations are to be avoided. There are a number of reasons why communication breaks down. The person's memory problem is one of the most important of these. The person forgets what he has already said and repeats the same remark over and over again. Or he or she forgets what you are talking about and starts talking about something quite irrelevant to the topic of conversation. This means that AD sufferers break all the 'rules' which we automatically follow in normal conversation, and this can lead to them appearing rude and self-centred; they don't follow the accepted convention of taking turns in a discussion. Or their memory problems lead them to forget some important detail—the age of the relative you are discussing, for example. They talk about your niece as if she were still at school when in reality she's now 50! Crossed wires abound in conversations with AD sufferers. Sometimes they will be unsure exactly who you are, and may assume you have some information that you do not possess, making it even harder to grasp their meaning. A sufferer may talk to her daughter as if they were together as children, for example, or she may address a visiting doctor as if she were aware of the ins and outs of the family tree.

Other problems arise from the speech centres in the person's brain not functioning properly. This can lead to a variety of difficulties with the expression and the understanding of language. The person may have problems in finding the right word, hesitating as an attempt is made to retrieve it. Or she may mix up words, even invent new ones to fill the gaps. The person may appear to know what he or she wants to say but not be able to put it into words—a frustrating experience for someone who was once articulate; in some severe cases, speech becomes an indistinct jumble of sounds. Other sufferers seem to lose understanding of what is said, perhaps misinterpreting the words, or simply failing to grasp their meaning. The more complex the communication is, the more likely this is to occur. In the most severe cases, it must feel to the sufferer that everyone else is speaking a foreign language—a bewildering experience of isolation and alienation, with only gesture and tone of voice giving clues to what is being said. Problems are not confined to spoken language; reading and writing skills may also be specifically impaired when particular areas of the brain are damaged. What can be done to help communication? There are several points to bear in mind.

Make sure the impact of any sensory problems is reduced as much as possible—spectacles and hearing aids are obviously helpful, but the reduction of background noise and good illumination may also reduce hearing and visual problems. If the sufferer needs dentures, make sure that he actually wears them and that they fit well! Remember also that the carer may have to take responsibility for ensuring that spectacles are clean, that the correct pair is worn for particular tasks, and that the hearing aid is switched on and has an effective battery. Deafness is not helped by shouting! Speaking clearly and distinctly is more helpful. Speaking to the better ear (where there is one), and making sure you don't mumble or cover your mouth with your hand when speaking, will also help.

Keep sentences short and simple enough to give the person the best chance of grasping what you are saying. If what you say is too long, the person may well forget by the end what you said at the beginning. If you use complicated sentences or unusual words, the person's ability to make sense of what is heard will be stretched, potentially beyond its reduced capability. For example, 'You're going to be taken later on, when she gets back from school, to the day-centre by Mary' demands more thought and memory than 'Later Mary will take you to the day-centre'. If the sufferer seems to be having trouble grasping what you say, it's well worth trying to speak more slowly and more simply, sticking to one idea at a time.

Use memory joggers to remind the person of the topic of

conversation. The spoken word literally vanishes without trace—it is there for a moment, then gone. It can be repeated, but it may still have little impact in a few seconds time. On the other hand, something concrete can give a tangible reminder of what you have been talking about. A picture, an object or something written may serve this purpose, depending on the situation and the person's abilities. Photographs of family and friends—both recent and from the past—can help with some discussions; a message board or a note-pad in a familiar place, a clear calendar or a diary to which reference can be made together with today's newspaper, can help keep track of recent events and forthcoming engagements. Don't merely talk about the bargain you've just bought—show the person!

Interesting events and people will stimulate conversation. It is much more likely to be rambling and disjointed when there is no focus, nothing to capture the attention from moment to moment. Carers often remark that the sufferer appears more alert when the doctor calls; indeed, sometimes they wonder whether anyone else really believes how disabled the person is. Make use of this by planning regular visits from people not so directly involved with caring. Their freshness and energy will help to hold the person's attention for a while longer than the everyday round of activities. Some sufferers respond well to young children and babies—making all the right noises and showing a lot of interest; some respond well to pets and animals, stroking and making a fuss of a dog or cat, for instance. The person's past interests play a part here, naturally enough. The point is that if the person has contact with people, things, or experiences that are of special individual interest, conversation and communication is more likely to flow than where there is little or nothing to stimulate and capture the person's attention.

Allow plenty of time—a good way to reduce anyone to incoherence and eventual silence is to rush him, or to interrupt before he or she has finished speaking, whilst speaking quickly yourself! You need to allow time for the person to understand what you are saying, time for him to respond adequately, time for you to make sense of what he or she is trying to say (which may differ from what is actually said). If the person cannot communicate his or her meaning to you, feelings of frustration are likely to be the result. Untangling what is said can be difficult and time-consuming—conversation with a dementia-sufferer can be hard work! Helping the person to feel relaxed and unpressured is a good way to bring out the best in him as a communicator.

Be aware of body language—yours and the patient's. Words are not the only vehicle of communication. Messages may also be given or received through body language. This may include the person's facial expressions, posture, tone and pitch of voice, and so on. Again, this is a two-way process. By observing the sufferer's body language, it may be possible to pick up additional clues to help you understand what the person is saying, or to help you assess whether what you are saying is being understood. The face usually provides most information—although, in certain instances, due perhaps to Parkinson's Disease or a stroke, the expressiveness of the face may be much reduced. You can also make use of your own body language to help you express more clearly and unambiguously the message you want to get across to the sufferer. Even if the words you use are not fully grasped, your tone of voice and facial expression may be perceived as warm, comforting and calming; a less careful approach may come across as aggressive, threatening or disturbing and lead to a completely different reaction! Speaking a little more slowly, a lower pitch, a softer tone—all these things will help make your voice more reassuring; a smile and a slow, open approach that gives the sufferer plenty of time to read your face, will help the person to feel less threatened.

The whole range of emotions—sadness, joy, anger, fear, disgust, surprise, warmth, hatred, bewilderment—can all be communicated without a word being said. AD sufferers are able to pick up the subtle signs that comprise this language, and in many instances will respond appropriately, given time—positively to joy and warmth, negatively to anger, disgust and hatred. A good way of appreciating the impact of body language on an AD sufferer is to think of the impact of first impressions. We look around on a train or bus and instantly have ideas about what other people are like, even though they are complete strangers to us. This impression comes largely from our reading of the stranger's body language—appearance, posture, expression, tone of voice, etc. Fortunately, when we get to know somebody we change our opinion—he's not really arrogant, just a bit shy; she's not really a miserable person, quite lively when she gets going. Our relationships would be very different if we relied only on those often erroneous and misleading first impressions. The AD sufferer has trouble in recognising people, getting to know them, remembering who and what they are, and so is very often in the situation of being approached by people who seem to the sufferer to be virtual strangers, although she may well be aware that the other person seems to know her. In this situation the sufferer can only evaluate the approaching person in terms of body language—at its most basic: friend or foe—because he does not have access to the background knowledge of the person that would help to make sense of the situation. This is more likely to happen with people outside the family; but as difficulty in recognising family members increases, so the importance of giving the correct 'first impression' through your own body language increases— when it is nearly all that the sufferer has to go on.

Use the past as a means of positive communication. Many sufferers are able to converse about past events—at times, it seems, with greater clarity than about the present day. This may show how well used we are to recalling events from the past. Conversations of this kind can be a possibility with many sufferers, particularly with the aid of photographs and mementoes of the people and events involved. In day-centres and hospitals, staff are using such reminders of the past more and more to stimulate conversation either on a one-to-one basis or with a group of sufferers. Often they use commercially available photographs, slides, tapes of music, voices and sounds from a particular period. At home, whilst you may not have access to materials of this kind, you probably have many reminders of the individual's own past. One way of using these is to make a 'This is your Life' album with the sufferer; this could document the landmarks and major events of the person's life, accompanied by relevant photographs, ration books, school certificates, etc. If some of the older pictures are rather small, making it hard to identify the people on them, they can often be enlarged at relatively little cost. A loose-leaf folder with clear plastic inserts in which photographs, documents and written material can be mounted, provides a suitable, durable and flexible album for this purpose. One advantage of such a book is that it can accompany the sufferer to the respite-care home or the day-centre and enable the sufferer to give the staff a very clear message about her own identity. This can prove a great aid to personalised care.

Some carers have been amazed at the extent to which a sufferer is able to recognise other people from photographs, some perhaps unknown to the carer himself. When life is now so potentially stressful, it can be refreshing to remember some of the moments that you have enjoyed together; for many of us these past memories can be a source of comfort and pleasure in difficult times—as long as we do not use them to reinforce how bad the present is in contrast to 'the good old days'. For some, the past has many unhappy moments, some traumatic, others involving regret and guilt. The aim is not to bring such events to the person's memory, of course, but to follow the sufferer's own lead: Respect the sufferer's wishes if he does not want to talk about something; but do not seek to avoid difficult topics of conversation deliberately. They are all part of the ups and downs of the person's life.

Try to make sense of what the person is trying to communicate. At times, it may seem nonsensical—random words or sounds that don't fit together or don't relate to the current situation. Before dismissing it as rubbish, however, it's always worth asking yourself whether the person is trying to tell you something but hasn't the words or the linguistic ability to get it across clearly. This is where observing the person's body language carefully can be a great help. Is the person in need of the toilet? Is he or she in pain? Does he or she feel insecure and worried? Is the person simply using a more familiar word for a new part of their life—'work' instead of 'day-centre'; 'mother' instead of 'daughter'? For the person with dementia, making sense of the new often means falling back on past experiences, so the person talks 'as if' he or she were in another phase of life. Recognising this can help you to understand that the person is not simply rambling, and allow you to tune in to the relevance of what the person is saying to the current situation. If the person is trying to communicate with you it's well worth taking the time and the trouble trying to understand both what he or she is saying, and—equally important—what he or she means.

Basic communication can mean a smile and a hug, a song and a dance! When language becomes very impaired, speech indistinct, and there seems to be little or no understanding, it is still possible (and important) to make person-to-person contact with the AD sufferer. Holding the person's hand, getting her attention by looking at her face-to-face (a powerful signal for communication to commence), using the person's name, are all good ways to initiate contact. Familiar music may produce a response where words fail—some sufferers with little or no speech can sing along with very familiar songs; the person's feet may start tapping; perhaps even a dance is possible. Love and warmth can be communicated through hugs and cuddles; helping the person to enjoy favourite foods is another way of showing love and concern. Chatting to the person even though little seems to be understood may communicate a feeling of togetherness—although it's surprisingly difficult for most of us when there is so little response. Taking the person for a walk relieves the pressure to talk and gives some feeling of a shared activity. Remember that even when your words seem to have little impact, the person may still be receiving the messages of your body language—ultimately the most basic communication is about needs and feelings. It may seem unsophisticated, but who is to say it is less valid than the conversation about nothing in particular which forms the bulk of communication for many of us in our day-to-day lives?

Routines can be helpful for all of us. They reduce the number of decisions we need to make. They help to bring order, structure and predictability into what could otherwise be chaotic daily lives. If there is no flexibility at all we may feel confined, unable to step off a tread-mill of habit and ritual; but to some degree—particularly when we are under stress and strain—most people find some regular pattern a help and a comfort. It enables us to operate on 'automatic pilot', conserving energy for important matters rather than frittering it away on the trivial daily round.

Having a regular pattern of care can then be tremendously

helpful in facing the daily challenges of caring for the AD sufferer. It can also help the sufferer because regularity and routine impose less of a day-to-day memory load; they come to represent familiarity and perhaps even security—especially if past routines are incorporated. Despite the memory problems, some AD sufferers will adjust to a new routine if it is repeated often enough. For instance, after a couple of weeks those twice-weekly visits to the day-centre become an accepted part of the person's life, and there is consternation if the pattern is broken by the transport not arriving! In caring for an AD sufferer it is important not to become a slave to routine, of course. As the person's condition changes the pattern of care will need to be thought through and modified with the changing circumstances and, if necessary, a new pattern established for a time until it too is perhaps overtaken by events. Unfortunately, providers of services do not always seem to appreciate the need for consistency, reliability and regularity to ease the load on both carer and sufferer. This is worth bearing in mind when you consider what services would be of real value to you. Can the service providers deliver a reliable, regular, predictable service on which you can depend? Most carers can well do without the disappointment and disruption of an unreliable service! Of course, nothing in this life can be 100 per cent reliable—delays occur, sickness or an accident may intervene—but at least there should be some contingency plan for the most predictable of the problems that are likely to arise. You need to know, for example, that if the day-centre transport is cancelled someone will visit the sufferer and arrange food and drink without you being called home from work in the middle of a busy morning. If the home-help is going on holiday, it's not unreasonable to expect to be told beforehand what arrangements will be made for this period. The best laid plans can and do go awry, and no routine will hold for ever, but a well thought-out structure, with some emergency back-up built in, can certainly be worthwhile in relieving the pressure of providing care.

Get all the help you can

Asking for help is not an admission of failure or of

weakness—it is a sensible strategy for dealing with a problem that is almost certain to get worse. It makes sense to have help arranged, to have supportive services well established, before you reach a point of overwhelming crisis. You may feel that you can manage at the moment, that there must be other carers in far greater need than yourself of the services that are available. Inevitably, at some point care will have to be shared, and the sooner this process begins the better for all concerned; it gives the sufferer time to adjust gradually to different people being involved, perhaps to going out to different centres; it gives the services a chance to get to know the sufferer gradually, perhaps whilst he is more able to communicate and share parts of his past life—much preferable to having to get to know the person in the midst of a crisis. Finally, it's better for the carer because the assumption and expectation (held by other family members, the sufferer and perhaps even the carer herself) that she will do everything is challenged right from the start, and this is undoubtedly in the best interests of the carer. The aim is surely to become the main organiser of care rather than the one who provides it all. Some carers feel selfish when they get others to do things that they could do without help. However, if the time released is used for the carer to relax, pursue one of their interests, maintain a career, then in the long run the sufferer will also benefit.

Getting help is, it must be said, not always easy. Who do you ask? Will they be sympathetic? What is available? In Chapter 7 some of the possible sources of help are listed; exactly what is available varies from area to area, of course. You may well need to be persistent in your requests. Many carers report that their family doctor is initially unhelpful, putting the problems down to 'old age' (whether the person is 60 or 90!). In such a situation you may find that other carers —met through the Alzheimer's Society or another group— can guide you through the system more readily. They may well have more knowledge and information of what is available locally than most of the professionals. They have already discovered their way through a system of services that may seem to you bewildering, confusing, contradictory in its complexity. They will have learned the hard way, so benefit from their experience. On the other hand, you yourself will have the best idea of how much support you can expect from family, friends and neighbours. Again, don't be afraid to ask; arrange a family meeting (see Chapter 3) so that everyone is clear about what help is needed. In every case it may be necessary to persist with your requests—don't give up if they don't immediately come up with the goods! Be clear about what you need—it's worth writing down a list of the difficulties you are facing. Although they may not always give this impression, the health and social services exist to provide a service to those with particular needs. Often they are restricted by limited resources, but from their point of view supporting someone who is caring for an AD sufferer at home is a very cost-effective use of their resources. Hospital or residential care is a very costly alternative. So you have no need at all to feel you're being a burden on the welfare services by asking for help—in many instances, it's really you who are doing them a favour!

Avoid confrontation

Part of maintaining a balance is to avoid putting undue pressure on the sufferer. For example, there is no point at all in asking the person questions you know they cannot answer, or in correcting them every time they say something that is incorrect. To be continually reminded of failure is likely to lead to frustration and feelings of humiliation. If the person gets in a mess whilst dressing, telling him off for putting his vest on over his shirt again will have no beneficial effect at all. Much better to supervise his dressing if this happens regularly giving enough prompting to make sure the clothes go on in the right sequence. And if it happens only occasionally, why make a scene about it? If the vest has to be removed, do it tactfully, perhaps saying, 'I've been looking for that vest everywhere—I need it in the wash so it's ready for you tomorrow.' In other words, try to avoid drawing unecessary attention to his failures. If the person wets his or her clothes, the important thing is to get the clothes changed calmly and smoothly. It is not uncommon for the person to deny the incontinence; perhaps to say that a drink must have been spilt or even that it was someone else's fault. Resist the temptation to argue: you will simply make the person aware of what she has done. This is especially difficult when it's the third accident that morning or if you took the person to the toilet with no result ten minutes before. Recriminations at this stage will serve little purpose and can simply make a difficult situation worse. Remember it is the disease, not the person, that is to blame. It is very difficult for the sufferer to retain any semblance of dignity—and if you can avoid pushing the person to a point where he or she feels the need to defend their dignity by becoming aggressive, this will be to the benefit of both of you.

Obviously a lot depends on the person and your relationship with them; if they're used to being the dominant partner, you will have to be very careful indeed to avoid confrontation. If the opposite is the case, a little more directness may be possible. Be warned, however, that most instances of aggression by people with AD arise from feelings of threat or where the person's failing abilities are challenged. When a person feels crowded, humiliated, uncertain of the intentions and good will of those surrounding him, he is much more likely to lash out with fist or foot in primitive self-defence.

If the person won't get up in the morning, why argue with them? If you do you will become more and more irritated, they will become more entrenched, and a confrontation will ensue. Why not try leaving them there and, returning ten minutes later with a cup of tea? This gives time for the earlier disagreement to be forgotten. This is not to say that in every case a head-on clash can be avoided, but some can—by careful planning and working around the difficulty so that the sufferer does not lose face.

Assess and minimise risks

Risks are an everyday part of life: accidents in the home are even more common than accidents on the roads. And as life becomes more complex, so the risks involved—for all the built-in safety-features—seem to multiply. People with AD run greater risks than most because of their disabilities—they are simply more likely to do dangerous things. Memory problems may lead to gas-taps not being turned off; poor judgement may lead to the person allowing unwelcome strangers into the home; poor practical skills may mean dangerous spills and scalds in the kitchen.

The only way to avoid all risks is to be wrapped up in cotton wool—not to go out; to avoid all dangerous substances; to be constantly monitored and checked... Yes, most people will agree that a life without risk would be no life at all! Yet each of us tries to reduce our own level of risk to what we consider an acceptable level—looking both ways when crossing the road; throwing away food when it passes the sell-by date; not keeping lemonade in weed-killer bottles; making sure that a ladder is secure before climbing it, and so on. The approach to the AD sufferer has to be based on the same principles. There will inevitably be some degree of risk, but as much as possible should be done to reduce the risks involved without being over-protective.

In practice, at least two different sorts of risks are involved. First, there is the risk of an awful event or crisis—the explosion, the fall, the fire, the robbery. The second kind is the risk of a gradual decline—from self-neglect, failure to take essential medication or to eat an adequate and nutritious diet, failure to drink sufficient quantities of fluid or to maintain one's personal hygiene. This kind of risk is perhaps a little easier to control. Once the danger has been spotted, the aim must be to ensure that the person has enough support and is monitored regularly to prevent such a decline occurring. This kind of risk is more likely if the AD sufferer lives alone. Where there is a carer on the spot, regular support and supervision can prevent risk of self-neglect. When the sufferer lives alone, it is important to mobilise the various local services into providing the sort of help that is needed.

Risk of a dangerous event is of course greater when the person lives alone, but accidents can happen just as easily when the sufferer lives with someone else. There must always be the possibility of something unforeseen occurring even if the home has been made as safe as possible—loose rugs removed, potentially dangerous liquids kept well away from food cupboards, medicines locked away, a guard put around an open fire, ash trays in every room if the person smokes, and so on. But if the person lives alone your efforts must be re-doubled. If the person is a danger with gas appliances, have the gas turned off and make alternative arrangements for heating and cooking. Sensible precautions *must* be taken. But not every danger can be anticipated, so it is important that the person is monitored regularly, and that all the various people involved— professionals, family, friends, neighbours—keep in close touch to assess any new risks that may develop, and work out ways of reducing their potential impact.

Risks do not come to an end when the person is in a home or a hospital. Where the person has difficulty walking, falls may occur. Should the person be restricted to a chair with a table across the front so that they cannot get up? In some homes and hospitals there have been instances of people being tied to chairs to prevent the risk of them getting up and falling. A balance has to be struck between preventing the dangers of falling (and possibly sustaining a serious fracture) and taking away a person's freedom altogether. These judgements can be very difficult to make. In many situations the thought of how guilty we would feel if something were to happen leads to our being over-protective. By and large the use of restraints is counter-productive; restlessness and agitation simply increase. On the other hand, giving people greater freedom may require more staff—to supervise unsteady walking or ensure that the person doesn't wander out of the ward.

And then there is the question of more subtle restraints. Medication may be used to reduce a person's restlessness, aggression or agitation, but most of the drugs used (the major tranquillisers for the most part) can have negative effects too. These may include excessive drowsiness and changes of blood pressure (which increases the risk of a fall). Again, a balance must be struck, using the minimum of medication to achieve the maximum positive effect with the least harmful side-effects.

A good home or ward will want to include the patient's family in any discussion about the degree of freedom and independence that is consistent with the patient's safety. This can only be worked out on an individual basis, and much may depend on the sufferer's own attitude. Some find any restriction so cumbersome that the painful and difficult decision to let the person fail at home, with all its attendant risks, must be taken. For some, this may actually shorten the person's life—a life of relative neglect at home simply cannot be compared with the care and nutritious food he or she would receive in a residential home. But there are those for whom this seems preferable. Others come to value the company and security of communal living once it is actually experienced. The decision to place restrictions on another human being can never be taken lightly even if we think we know that it's for the person's own good. One of the tragedies of AD is how frequently these decisions must be taken. Reducing risk with the minimum of restriction must be the guiding principle.

When to correct the person?

The person with AD will make many mistakes—about people and names (their own included), where they are and what is happening to them; about times, dates and the passage of time; about the sequence of events; about the reasons for what is going on around them. Carers often ask whether they are 'doing wrong' by 'going along' with ideas they know to be incorrect. Some are concerned that they may be going against the principles of 'reality orientation'. This is an approach used by a number of professionals working with people who suffer from dementia which, from its name at least, seems to place an emphasis upon putting the person right, orientating them to 'reality'. In fact, the golden rule of reality orientation is not to *agree* with statements the persons says which are incorrect. This is quite different from correcting the person on each and every occasion. There are parents who cannot stop themselves correcting their children every time they mispronounce a word or make a grammatical error. There are teachers who make a fuss about the slightest spelling mistake. The result is often a resentful or withdrawn child who finds that efforts at self-expression are stifled, not rewarded. The same may happen to an AD sufferer who is constantly corrected.

How can these two aims of not agreeing with incorrect ideas and yet avoiding correcting the person constantly be achieved? One strategy that can help in many situations is simply to change the subject and talk about something else. This prevents you becoming embroiled either in disagreeing with the sufferer or in agreeing with something that you know is not true. A second strategy is to agree with the parts that you know to be accurate, and try to catch the overall sense of what the person is attempting to communicate. If the sufferer's daughter (Jean) is expected any minute, but the sufferer seems to be on the look-out for her own mother, you might guess that 'mother' and 'daughter' are being mixed up. You could then say, 'I expect Jean will be here in a minute', rather than explain to the sufferer that mother died ten years ago... The sufferer knows someone is due, so respond to that rather than to the inaccurate part of the statement.

Some people feel uncomfortable if they do not respond to the false components of what the person says, feeling that it is always important to be completely truthful. In fact, we are always making decisions about how much of 'the truth' should be imparted at any particular time. The whole truth is often painful and difficult for the AD sufferer because it draws attention to the disintegration of their abilities. Any correction should be offered in a way that helps the person to save face; gently assisting them to rediscover the facts rather than emphasising the carer's superior knowledge and abilities. This can be achieved by reference to memory aids (see next section) or by highlighting the carer's own fallible faculties. You might say, for example, 'I think it's Tuesday today, but we'd better check the calendar—since I retired every day seems the same.' If you feel you have to correct the sufferer, do it gently, tactfully, carefully. If the sufferer has been bereaved and continues to talk about the dead person as if he or she were still alive, be aware that when you correct the person, it may seem a little like the first time the news has been broken to them. You need to be prepared for the normal emotional reaction on a number of occasions. Little by little the idea that the person has gone will begin to gain some familiarity.

In some ways, the person may be thought of as having lost the time-chart that gives each of us a clear idea of where we are in life—what is past, current, or planned for the future. Sometimes the sense of lostness is so great that it is not precise, minute detail that the person needs but a rough guide as to where they are; not that mother died 20 years ago, but that she is not here now; not that they left work ten years ago, but that today is not a working day. The whole truth, with its wealth of detail and precision, its awful revelation of the reasons for the lapses of memory, is usually not what is needed—rather, just enough to help the person make some sense of the current situation. Of course, sometimes the sufferer requests more detail, and this may present an ideal opportunity for more of the gaps to be filled—temporarily. It is much preferable for this to be at the sufferer's own request, under her own control, and absorbed at her own pace.

Using memory aids

Most people use memory aids at one time or another. Watches and clocks help us to keep track of the time; calendars and diaries remind us of the day, the date, the appointments we must keep. Maps and signs help us to find our way around an unfamiliar town or a large building. When we are really busy we make a list of all the tasks we have to get finished. Some of us tie a knot in a handkerchief when we have something important to remember; many of us remember how many days there are in each month by reciting the rhyme we learned in school.

It is only too evident that if those of us blessed with 'normal' memory find it hard to remember things without an aid of some kind, the needs of the AD sufferer must be all the greater. The question is, of course, to what extent the sufferer is actually able to make use of these strategies. Several points need to be considered.

First, there is little point in relying on memory aids that add to the memory load. The familiar knot in the handkerchief is fine if we are able to remember why we put it there in the first place! The alarm going off on your watch may be a good reminder—but of what? Reminders need to be specific to the task in hand, reducing rather than adding to the memory load. Secondly, familiar aids and associations are usually more effective than new ones—a familiar type of diary, for example, or lists in places where the sufferer previously kept them. If it is familiar, it removes the necessity for the sufferer to learn how to use it. Thirdly, the aid needs to give the information in a manner that can be easily grasped by the sufferer. This means a calendar where today's date is clearly given, explicitly picked out from the other days of the month; the diary must have today's entry marked. If signs are used to help the person avoid getting lost around the house, they should be clear and give the information in a word or a picture that the sufferer already understands. For example, many do not recognise some of the modern symbolic signs for 'toilet'; here, the word most familiar to the particular person would be most effective. Signs and notices should use clear lettering in colours that stand out so that the aid may be seen and used even under poor lighting conditions. It may seem unnecessary to mention that if clocks, calendars and other aids are used they must be accurate! Unfortunately, clocks giving the wrong time and notices giving out-of-date information are only too frequently seen in hospitals and old people's homes.

Many AD sufferers do have some ability to learn. For instance, after a few weeks in hospital the sufferer may have learned to find the toilet; after some months at the day-centre, the sufferer may know the name of a favourite staff member. This learning ability can be used to advantage in some instances, although, as previously stated, it is always preferable to avoid adding further to the sufferer's memory load. Sometimes a little new learning allows the use of a potentially effective aid, and so can be well worth the effort involved. Where this is the case, simplicity, consistency and repetition are called for. Simplify the information required as far as possible; make a routine of using the information in the same way on each occasion; be prepared to repeat the procedure many times before there is any indication that it is beginning to sink in! A good example would be teaching the sufferer always to keep her purse, handbag or wallet in a particular place; or to encourage him to read the check-list by the door before leaving for the day-centre (check for your key; turn off lights; lock back door).

If the person lives alone, or is left for long periods during the day, a valuable aid can be a list of visitors expected (home-help, neighbours, for example), who then mark off the list when they arrive and leave. This helps the sufferer (and the carer) keep track of who has been to the house and who is still to call. The notice needs to be in a prominent place (on a notice-board in the kitchen, for example, or wherever the sufferer tends to sit). It must be up-dated regularly, and the various visitors reminded of its importance. A list of useful telephone numbers, fixed securely to the telephone, may also be helpful for some sufferers.

If you live with the sufferer and are going out, it may help to leave a note saying where you have gone and when you are due back (give yourself some leeway in case you miss the bus!). A chart of the day's events and their times, ticked off as they are completed, also helps the sufferer to deal with the difficulty of keeping track of time.

Pictures of various family members (as they are now) may be displayed prominently, clearly labelled to help the sufferer keep track of who's who. It helps if the pictures are fairly large and are good likenesses! A family scrapbook might serve a similar purpose. Again, clear labels are required. The sufferer may well not remember everyone's name.

Finally, it can be very frustrating when important items—keys, handbag, spectacles or purse, for example—go missing. Hours can be spent hunting high and low. One strategy is always to keep such articles in the same places. Another is to ensure that they are easy to see; the spectacle case might have a piece of coloured tape attached to it; the keys could be attached to a large key ring. Some key rings have a device which enables them to respond to a whistle so that they can be found in the dark.

Ensure that spare keys are readily available, and that family treasures and really valuable items are safely locked away. Discovering the person's favourite hiding places can save a lot of time. Sufferers hide articles for 'safety' in the oddest of places—and then forget where they have hidden them!

Chapter Five

Coping with day-to-day life

Bathing and hygiene

This is an area where great tact and diplomacy is needed. The AD sufferer may simply forget to attend to personal hygiene. Yet, like most of us, any suggestion to this effect will be met with shock or resentment. Later, as skills as well as memory decline, the person's ability to carry out the tasks required may be lost; the problem then becomes one of how to cater for another person's most intimate hygiene in a way that allows a semblance of dignity to be retained on all sides. Safety issues also arise, especially in relation to bathing.

For some, gentle reminders of the need to have a regular routine of washing and bathing at certain times will be enough. As time goes on, discreet monitoring may become increasingly necessary to ensure the wash is carried out adequately and that clothes are being changed regularly. When motivation seems to be dwindling, ensure there is something for which it is worth being well groomed—the day-centre or going out to the pub, for instance. Make sure the sufferer receives lots of compliments when she is well turned out or has a new hair-do. Good grooming can of course help self-esteem tremendously; if the person has been used to paying regular visits to the hairdresser, or has always enjoyed having nicely manicured nails, try to continue these activities as far as possible, emphasising how nice it is to be pampered if the person has to be less actively involved than before.

In this area, as others, try to avoid confrontation; use praise and encouragement. Don't nag the person to have a wash or criticise his standards of cleanliness. For some, a degree of choice may help. 'When would you prefer to have a bath—this morning or this evening?' still carries the message that it's going to be today! Others can accept the decision being made for them: 'I've run a nice bath for you. You usually have one before you go to bed.' If the person is reluctant, try first thing in the morning or last thing at night when the person will be undressed anyway. Some sufferers seem fearful of a full bath—a lower water level may be more acceptable. Use bath foams and other 'smellies' to help bath-time to be an enjoyable experience rather than a chore. Ensure the bathroom is warm and inviting. There are times when no choice can be allowed, of course—the person simply has to be cleaned up, perhaps after incontinence. Here you must be firm; there is a job that has to be done which may well be unpleasant for both parties. There's no point in criticising the person for the accident, however irritating or inconvenient it may be. The calmer you can remain, the more likely the clean-up operation is to be completed quickly and efficiently. The person probably feels humiliated enough at losing this basic control of bladder or bowel—although it's not unusual for the person to deny responsibility altogether, or to be strangely unaware, perhaps as a defence against the awful realisation of loss of control.

When direct supervision has to be given, allow the person to do whatever he or she can unaided; if the difficulty is mainly in following the necessary sequence of tasks, verbal reminders may be sufficient, and laying out the soap, face cloth and towel may also help. Even when more physical help is needed, the person can still be encouraged to carry out the parts of the wash of which he or she is still capable. If you give the person a soaped flannel, he or she may well be able to wash some parts of the body, leaving you to help with the rest.

Safety is important, and can be used as a legitimate reason for unobtrusive supervision. Water temperature should be checked before the person gets in the bath. It's worth making sure that water from the hot-water system doesn't come out scalding hot (usually there is a thermostat that can be adjusted on the hot water boiler). In the bath, a non-slip bath mat is essential. Bath aids to help the person get in and out of the bath may be needed; a hand-grip fixed firmly to the wall or a bath seat may be appropriate. Information can be obtained from an occupational therapist, who will also advise you on how to obtain the aids recommended. Contact with an OT can be made through your local social services office. For some, a shower may be helpful, especially in dealing with incontinence. People vary in their preferences, and some older people may not be happy with a shower. For others it can be very helpful and the right sort of shower unit can avoid many of the difficulties of helping a fairly immobile person in and out of a bath. The person may be much more able to step in and out of a shower tray; it is also possible to sit on a chair of normal height in the shower. Several carers looking after severe AD sufferers have said what a boon a shower unit has been. If the occupational therapist recommends it, it is sometimes possible to have one fitted through the Social Services department; if you can afford it, you may avoid a long wait.

For men, increasing help may be needed with shaving. Many carers prefer to use an electric razor rather than have a wet shave. However, a co-operative sufferer may still appreciate a wet shave if he had previously used this method. Hairdressing is important for men and women; if the person can no longer go to the hairdresser it may be possible to find one who will come to the home; or the day-centre may have facilities for this aspect of personal care. Chiropody is important in maintaining the person's mobility; if there are any problems with the person's feet or nails a chiropodist should be consulted. Again, some make home visits or carry out sessions at day-centres. The chiropody service is provided by the Health Service and may be contacted through your family doctor; or you may see a chiropodist privately. Dental care is important in relation to feeding and communication, and the person should be encouraged to continue with dental hygiene, cleaning their own teeth or dentures as appropriate. Again, it is easiest if this is built into the daily routine.

While helping the person in the bath, it is worth looking out for areas of skin that are becoming red and sore, usually from the pressure associated with insufficient exercise. The base of the back and the heels are among the areas most commonly affected. You will need medical help if pressure sores develop, with regular visits from a nurse, who will advise on how the areas should be treated and what preventative measures may be taken.

As stated at the outset, personal hygiene is a delicate matter. It may be that you and the sufferer have always had different standards. You like to shower twice a day; he or she always had a bath once a week. There is no doubt that if you try to impose your standards on the sufferer, you will meet resistance. It may be better to ensure the daily wash is adequate than make this area a battleground. Some older people never bath, preferring to have a good strip-down wash. Some have never had a bathroom, so they have never had the choice! Building on the person's past routines is more likely to be successful than instituting a completely new regime. For some carers, the relationship they have with the sufferer is such that they may feel unable to be involved in bathing or washing the person. In many areas a bath attendant is available who will help the sufferer to bathe at home. Some day-hospitals and day-centres will help also with bathing. Such help is relatively infrequent, however; bath attendants may call as little as once or twice a fortnight. Sometimes district nurses will be able to help with washing the person on a regular basis, as will those home-helps who have a personal care role.

Dressing

Once again, the basic strategy is to give just enough help to enable the sufferer to carry out as much of the task independently as possible. It's important first of all to allow sufficient time so that neither you nor the sufferer becomes flustered through feeling rushed. Then try to foresee any situations where the person might get the clothes mixed up or otherwise get themselves in a mess whilst dressing. For some, this means laying out the clothes in the correct sequence (dress before cardigan); for others, ensuring night-clothes are removed before day-clothes are made available, or being ready to help when the garment is reached which you know cannot be put on unaided. Holding back to allow the person to be independent is fine, but allowing the person to become trapped inside a blouse or a shirt is counter-productive. Trying to remove clothes once they are on (because you think the vest looks better under the dress!) does not get the day off to a good start.

Verbal reminders may help. As skill declines, it may be necessary to think of the task as a series of small steps, some of which the sufferer can carry out with a little help. You may need to say, 'Put your arm through this hole here' rather than 'Put your jacket on now'. This step-by-step approach makes for simpler instructions, and allows the carer to give the minimum of physical help, even though the task as a whole would be quite beyond the sufferer.

When the sufferer is in difficulties, remember that AD may have the effect of taking away the person's ability to place their arms or legs in the places where they want them to go. It may prevent the person recognising clothes as clothes, or telling one garment from another. It is perfectly obvious to all but the AD sufferer that trousers do not go over the head... Always remember to blame the disease and not the sufferer.

Think of some simple solutions. Would the task be simpler if the shirt had larger buttons? Would smooth-running zip fasteners or velcro pull-apart fastenings help? The latter can be a godsend for those whose fingers are not deft enough to manage buttons or zips. Slip-on shoes are usually easier than those with laces or buckles; tights may be easier than stockings. Fastenings at the front will be easier for many. Men should never have button flies—far too fiddly for most sufferers! Easy-to-wash clothes are very important—especially if the person is incontinent or tends to be a messy eater. Clothes should be chosen carefully to help the person feel pleased with his or her appearance. They can contribute greatly to self-esteem. Clothes that look good even after repeated laundry are ideal. It is a good idea to remove dirty clothes from the person's room in the evening, so that they are not able to put them on again next day!

A few sufferers frequently undress during the day; it is worth checking to make sure the clothes are not too tight or uncomfortable in some other way. Otherwise, trying to distract them by suggesting more constructive activities is recommended. Some sufferers put on layer after layer of clothing (three dresses, two cardigans and a jumper, for instance!). Keeping most of the person's clothes inaccessible would be one way of tackling this difficulty, or there may be a simpler solution. Perhaps the person feels cold and needs warmer clothing.

Occasionally, in cases of some difficulty and disability, help with dressing and undressing can be obtained from district nursing staff or a home-help whose job includes personal care.

Meal-times

The ability to feed oneself is usually one of the last skills lost in AD. What may be considered good table manners or social graces, on the other hand, are not usually so well retained. A relaxed, sociable atmosphere can help; the sufferer will do better if not rushed. Distractions can be especially difficult for some sufferers at meal-times. They may be confused if anything apart from their meal is on the table in front of them. In such cases it is important to serve only one course at a time, have only essential utensils on the table, offer condiments and then remove them, and, if necessary, have a drink after rather than with the meal. If you know the person tends to be messy, ensure you use a wipe-down place mat or table cloth (many attractive plastic cloths are now available), and provide napkins to protect clothing as a matter of routine. Try to ensure the food is not too hot; the sufferer may not be able to judge the temperature safely. Some spillages may be prevented by not over-filling cups and glasses.

Plan the menu to suit the person's level of eating skill. He or she may look quite competent with a meal made up of bite-size chunks of (say) meat and vegetables, whereas a more difficult meal—fish on the bone, for example—might cause major difficulties. Food that is easy to cut up and manage will help the person to retain his independence. As skills deteriorate, less use of a knife and more use of a spoon may also help, as long as food is well cut up in advance. Eventually, finger foods such as sandwiches, chips and small pieces or raw vegetables or fruit may help the person to feed even when utensils cannot be used.

Aim for a balanced diet, ensuring plenty of fibre (use wholemeal bread, for example), protein, vegetables and fruit, with lots of fluids. If, like many sufferers, the person develops a sweet tooth and would prefer to eat only the puddings and sweets, try to use these as an incentive for eating some of the main course. If the person is reluctant to eat, serve small portions of the person's favourite dishes, but be careful not to over-pressurise the person or further resistance might develop. In extreme cases, where the person is losing weight through not eating, medical advice should be sought. In some cases vitamins or other diet supplements may be prescribed to compensate for the person's inadequate food intake.

A number of feeding aids are available; again, the occupational therapist is the best person to advise on these. These include non-slip mats to ensure that the plate does not move around the table; cutlery with thick handles for those with poor grip; feeder cups for those who shake too much to use an ordinary cup; plate guards, which fit around the plate and help the person scoop up food one-handed. All these aids aim to help the person preserve his independence. Adequate dentures are also important so that the person can chew and eat a range of textures of food. If dentures are loose, dental advice should be sought.

If the person does need to be fed, soft, thick food may be preferable; some sufferers forget to swallow, and must be reminded to do so because of the risk of choking. If you can hold the spoon in the person's hand and guide her through the motions of self-feeding, this can sometimes help to initiate part of the feeding sequence. If the person seems to hold the lips tightly closed when the spoon approaches, this may seem like a clear refusal; in fact, it may imply an involuntary reflex. In such instances, you must seek guidance from a nurse as to how best to proceed.

Meals on wheels, delivered to the person's home, or a meal at a day-centre, are the usual solutions to the problem of meals for AD sufferers living alone. In some places, neighbours can be paid to provide a meal on a regular basis. Of course, it is important to check that the meal is actually eaten and not left to go mouldy! A home-help or some other shopper may be able to keep the person's fridge and larder stocked with snacks, bread and cereals, for other meal-times. Much depends on how ingrained the meal-time routine is for sufferers who live on their own.

Sleep

By and large, older people tend to sleep less than younger

people; to have more broken sleep; to need to go to the toilet more often during the night; and to have more naps during the day. In AD sufferers, sleep may be particularly disturbed. The person gets up during the night, perhaps to use the toilet, but then does not settle back to sleep. Perhaps under the misapprehension that it is already morning, the person starts to get dressed, thinking it is time to go to the shops or to work. Or the person may get lost in the house; he may wander into the room of another family member and create havoc by getting into the wrong bed! One of the problems in coping with such problems is that few of us are at our best when woken in the middle of the night. It takes us a little while to come round, get to grips with the situation, initiate action. It is difficult not to respond in an irritated, short-tempered way. As the disturbance continues night after night the effects mount up; fatigue and weariness take hold; one's reserves of patience and resilience are eaten away; it is no wonder that again and again carers have reported regular disturbances at night as being the most difficult of the common problems to tolerate.

What can help? If (and it's a big if, of course) you can lead the person gently back to bed, speaking softly and soothingly, emphasising it's still the middle of the night, this is more likely to lead to the person going back to sleep than an angry response. If the person needs the toilet at night, ensure that the route is clearly lit; or perhaps a bed-side commode could be used. A night-light may help prevent the person becoming more confused on waking.

Ensuring that the person's clothes are not readily accessible may prevent him getting dressed in the middle of the night—persuading the person to get undressed again can be a major undertaking! Dark, heavy curtains in the person's bedroom can help prevent premature waking in the summer. Keeping the person awake and as active as possible during the day, with exercise and fresh air, will also contribute to a better night's sleep. A number of sufferers benefit from sleeping medication, although this should be monitored carefully to ensure that the person does not have a 'hangover'—drowsiness and a tendency to fall asleep—the following morning. This could indicate that the dosage is too high; or the medication might be given earlier in the evening.

It's worth trying to develop a familiar bed-time routine, helping the person to wind down and prepare for sleep; but bear in mind that most sufferers will not naturally sleep for more than seven or eight hours at the most. There is little point in trying to get the sufferer to bed very early (however much you may wish for the peace and quiet). Ensure the routine includes a visit to the toilet. A bed-time drink can be soothing, although drinks with caffeine, such as tea and coffee, are best avoided if sleep is a problem. The caffeine can act as a stimulant. Although carers are often advised to restrict fluids in the evening, there is no real evidence this reduces incontinence. Making sure the person is comfortable, not too hot or too cold, is also an important part of the bed-time routine. For some sufferers, the evening is a time of particular agitation and restlessness—perhaps because the carer is more tired, other family members have come in from work or there is less happening. Aim to have some ways of keeping the person quietly occupied in the evening—relaxing music, some ironing or cooking, watching a favourite TV programme together—so that the person is fairly calm and peaceful when bed-time arrives. If the person is very reluctant to go to bed, some carers have compromised and let the person sleep in a comfortable armchair, suitably covered with blankets.

It is a great shame that relatively little help is available at night from the social services. Sometimes a voluntary or a private agency can provide a night-sitter who will relieve the carer of responsibility for a time. The carer—equipped with ear plugs if necessary—can then get a good night's sleep. Unfortunately, such services are yet few and far between, and night time problems tend to fall mainly upon family and friends.

Social life

There are two ways in which your social life may be affected by being a carer. You may have shared your social life with the sufferer—as in the case of many husbands and wifes. Here the onset of AD may prevent the sufferer being able to continue as before. Or the need to care for the person may get in the way of your own participation in social events.

In the latter case, it is vital not to let your social life, friendships and relationships, be destroyed by your role as a carer. You will need outlets such as these to survive, times when you can relax and forget the problems for a few hours. If you cannot leave the person alone, you will need to find someone to come and stay with the person whilst you go out. Some voluntary organisations may be able to help with this; or you might consider asking a neighbour or another family member to help in this way. If the person has periods in a home or hospital to give you a break, make full use of this opportunity to visit friends, go to the theatre or whatever. If the person goes to a day-centre and you are at home during the day, arrange to see friends or family during the day, so that you have some time when you can keep your relationships alive and strong. They are an invaluable asset; you must treasure and preserve them.

If your social life was shared, you may now have to begin to develop your own. It can be difficult making new friends if in the past you had few outside contacts; adult education classes or clubs based on a particular activity or interest provide a good way of meeting others with similar interests. Your local Alzheimer's Society branch will also help put you in contact with others in a similar position; but you may decide you need a complete break from the disease at times.

If you had a healthy social life with your partner in the past, it may be possible to adapt the previous pattern a little to match the changed circumstances. If you went out regularly together to a pub, a restaurant or a club, it can take a lot of courage to continue unless the person has few problems that show outwardly. The cinema and the theatre require you to sit still for a considerable period of time; it can be very difficult to leave during the performance. Some sufferers may find the darkness confusing; most will not be able to follow the plot, of course. Concerts require long periods of sitting quietly, although the music itself may be enjoyed. A restaurant may be possible for some sufferers, although access to toilets, the general atmosphere, and how crowded the place is, will be important factors. If the sufferer needs help in the toilet and is of the opposite sex, accompanying the person can cause embarrassment; public places with facilities for the disabled are likely to be easier to manage. Visits to the pub may be possible, especially if it is fairly quiet and has a genuinely welcoming atmosphere. It may be worth going with someone else—a friend or family member—so that the full responsibility for the sufferer does not fall upon you for the whole time. Inviting friends to your home may prove easier than going to theirs—at least the sufferer will be on familiar ground, and you will have no need to worry about the person causing a mess. The sufferer will probably be able to cope best with small gatherings. Make sure visitors are forewarned about the problems, and advise them how best to converse with the sufferer—perhaps nostalgically recalling the past, or concentrating on topics that are fairly concrete and not too demanding. You may be able to help by filling in gaps, or gently and quietly prompting the sufferer when you feel that he or she is about to flounder. This can help the sufferer to enjoy the company without feeling completely inadequate or overwhelmed.

It is often said that in dire circumstances we find who are our real friends. Many carers report that friends tend to keep away, perhaps because they are embarrassed and don't know what to say to the sufferer. Some have even said that they would rather remember the sufferer as he or she used to be rather than be confronted by this changed person. If you can feel charitable towards such friends, remember that these attitudes often arise from ignorance of the sufferer's condition and your needs, or both. Some will be potentially educable—give them literature, invite them to Alzheimer Society meetings, point out relevant TV programmes. Ask them to do specific, concrete things—come and play cards with the sufferer, accompany him on a short walk, look together at the family photograph albums, for example. Some friends will of course be lost, but by being assertive, direct and clear in your requests to your friends early on, and by offering some basic information about the sufferer's condition, you may be fortunate enough to recruit valuable help and support. And by making specific requests, you may counter any feelings the friends have that they might be sucked into a situation where too many demands were being made of them. They will feel less helpless and useless if you can identify specific areas, things they can do to help. Some may be of most use as a support for you, offering a sympathetic ear when needed, even if they cannot help directly with the sufferer.

Exercise ȷ

Regular exercise is now recognised to be important for all of us, although it is vital not to do too much too soon. Exercise is of benefit to AD sufferers for a number of reasons: it will help reduce the chances of the person becoming constipated; it will help the person to sleep better; it will have a positive impact on their general health and reduce the danger of pressure sores which are often associated with lack of mobility.

The challenge comes in trying to find methods of exercise which are acceptable to the person, and in which he or she is capable of participating. Many younger sufferers remain physically fit for some time and it is important to harness their energy constructively. Much depends on the person's previous activities. Walking is often possible—in the country or a park; younger sufferers have continued to swim for a while; dancing is popular with many; the less active may manage movement to music or simple physical exercises which could involve imitating your movements, and may even be carried out sitting down if necessary. Some older sufferers may join in just to keep you company.

Recreation

The guiding principles here are to maintain and build on previous interests and activities; to adapt and simplify tasks so that the person is still able to manage them, albeit with help, supervision and encouragement; and to work within the person's now more limited concentration span and capabilities, reducing the demands made by the activity so that it becomes less difficult, less complex, and quicker to complete.

In practice, this means that many sufferers can continue their involvement with cooking or gardening, for example. Where the person once planned menus and catered for dinner parties without help of any kind, he or she may now be able to peel vegetables if asked to do so and provided with the appropriate utensils; or perhaps they could even bake a cake if they were given step-by-step reminders. At more severe levels of impairment, the person may just enjoy sitting in the kitchen, stirring the cake mixture perhaps, enjoying the smell of cooking, or tasting the food as it is being prepared. In the garden, the person may no longer be able to run a greenhouse or plan where to plant vegetables and flowers; but he may manage a little digging or sowing, under supervision. At any level of impairment the colours and fragrance of the flowers in a garden may still be enjoyed. Properly supervised, the sufferer may be able to water the house-plants or help grow tomato plants from seed. Before leaving the sufferer alone in the garden, however, ensure that there are no dangerous substances such as weed killer accessible that might conceivably be confused for something else. You may remember that the old lemonade bottle contains white spirit, but the sufferer will not! In both kitchen and garden, the sufferer's involvement may be much less than before, but the results can still be very worthwhile.

Other activities might include simple card games, dominoes, bingo, draughts, and even chess if the person had once been a practised player. Dominoes may be simplified by abandoning the points-scoring system, using larger dominoes or ones with a different colour for each number. Bingo may be shortened by having fewer numbers, using pictures instead of numbers, and by ensuring that there is a simple way of marking the numbers (or pictures) that have been called out. Some sufferers can manage simple crosswords or other word puzzles (making as many words as possible from the letters of a given long word, for example).

Craft and art work may be continued, although the results may be coarser and less skilful than before. The person may need more help to follow a knitting pattern; or she may move from knitting superb clothes to blanket squares. Clay modelling has proved possible for some sufferers. The aim is to find activities the person finds enjoyable and stimulating, although new activities might achieve a better response if introduced by someone other than the carer. Reading skills will naturally decline as the person finds it harder and harder to remember the plot and characters in the book. Short stories, magazines and newspapers may still be possible; very familiar stories might be re-read with the aid of a book-mark—the person will not remember the point in the story that has been reached.

Music is a recreation that may be enjoyed relatively

passively. Some sufferers continue to play a musical instrument, such as the piano, although in time this skill may also be lost. The ability to sing along with old, familiar tunes is often well-retained. Music can often get through to a sufferer when everything else has failed. Track down the person's favourite pieces of music; prepare a tape to accompany the person into respite care so that she does not have to listen to the current pop songs on the hospital radio.

The sufferer is more likely to be an armchair sports enthusiast than an active participant. Some sufferers certainly continue to play darts, snooker or bowls, but usually in a more sheltered environment where the person is not also obliged to maintain the level of social skills required in many sports. thus the person may play darts with family or friends, or at the day-centre, but not with the local pub league any more. Some sufferers will enjoy their sport on TV. Others can no longer concentrate for long and soon lose interest. Generally speaking, sufferers seem to enjoy TV programmes that are not too taxing: cartoons, Laurel and Hardy, Fred Astaire movies, for example. A very few sufferers are actually disturbed by TV, becoming unable to distinguish what is really happening in the room from what is happening on the screen. This can be very frightening in some instances—when gunmen are perceived as being in your living room, for example. Swift use of the 'off' button is recommended here.

Some sufferers are all too painfully aware of the poor performances they now achieve in long-standing activities. Some painters, for example, refuse to paint because the results are no longer satisfying. If all efforts at encouragement fail—including praise for effort rather than achievement—it may simply be kinder to move onto other activities than continue to press the person into a situation which seems to reinforce their feelings of failure.

Driving

If the sufferer has been driving for many years or has been the main driver in the family, this can become a major area of difficulty. For the simple fact of the matter is that people who have been diagnosed as suffering from AD or other dementias *must not* drive. It is tempting to think that as long as someone is with the person to ensure that they do not get lost everything will be alright. Or perhaps it seems safe to assume that local journeys on familiar routes will be OK. The problem is that unexpected incidents and accidents can happen just as readily on short, familiar routes as elsewhere and it is these with which the sufferer will have difficulty in coping, however well learned and habitual the ordinary skills of driving may be. The sufferer's reactions and judgement will have been impaired to some extent by the AD.

In the UK, your family doctor should contact the Driver and Vehicle Licensing Centre at Swansea—doctors have a legal duty to report any lasting disability (as AD undoubtedly is) to the licensing authority. Try to discuss this problem with the sufferer in a way that helps the person not to lose face too much. Sugar the pill if possible by blaming the person's poor vision or his reduced mobility. Mention the increasing amount of traffic or tell him that *you* would like to drive for a change—or whatever explanation seems reasonable and acceptable. Some sufferers will be relieved to relinquish the responsibility of driving; others will find this early sign of failing capabilities particularly depressing. Here some figure of authority—the family doctor or a local policeman, for example—may be able to lay down the law in a way which the family cannot. Ultimately, it may be necessary to hide the car keys or even immobilise the car (by removing the distributor cap or wire—a garage will show you how) to prevent the sufferer driving.

If you are able to drive, you may be able to claim a mobility allowance (for sufferers under 65 who have difficulty with walking); with older sufferers, it is possible to claim exemption from road tax. A disabled driver badge will prove useful in making parking easier; it may be claimed from your local Council if the sufferer has major problems with walking. If you cannot drive, one of the transport schemes for disabled people may be able to help. These have been set up in some places in recent years, using specially adapted vehicles to operate a low-cost taxi service for disabled people. The regularly updated *Disability Rights Handbook* will give details of such benefits as the Mobility Allowance; your local

Alzheimer Society branch should be aware of transport schemes in your area.

Holidays

Carers are often advised not to take AD sufferers on holiday—the unfamiliarity of the new place and the change of routine may prove too confusing. It may also be more difficult to get the help you need in an emergency than at home. Some sufferers find a long journey difficult and tiresome.

However, a number of carers have organised successful holidays with the sufferer by reducing potential problems to a minimum. This means going somewhere which is familiar to you both, a place where you know what to expect. If possible, preferably go with friends or other members of the family so that the responsibility of caring can be shared. Take plentiful supplies of medication and other necessities (incontinence pads, for example). Self-catering accommodation in a flat or a house may feel less like a real holiday, but it could involve less disruption of the person's routine. Caravans may be rather claustrophobic, allowing little space away from the sufferer; touring holidays, with a constant change of scene, are a non-starter. Staying with family or close friends where there is a real home-from-home feeling may be worth a try. If the holiday does involve a long journey, take plenty of things to occupy the person, and let the various helpers take it in turns to sit with him.

Some carers' groups have organised holidays together, taking over a small hotel or guest house for a week or so. Additional volunteer helpers have helped to ease the load on each carer. This has proved quite successful, and it certainly helps to overcome the embarrassment a carer might feel when alone with the sufferer in a hotel.

You must ask yourself whether going with the sufferer will give you, the carer, a holiday. Every carer needs regular holidays—for refreshment, revival and renewal. Would it be better for all concerned if you went on holiday without the sufferer? There are several options for the sufferer whilst you are away: respite care in a home or a hospital (depending on the person's difficulties); having someone come and stay with the person in the family home—another member of the family perhaps. Or the person may go away himself to a home that provides short-term holiday breaks—some social services departments operate such holiday homes, and a number of private ones are also in operation in holiday resorts. Which option you choose depends on the disability of the sufferer and the resources available to you. Having someone to stay with the person may be the least disruptive, especially if it is someone familiar.

Sex

If physical affection was an important part of your relationship in the past, there is no reason why it should not continue. The sufferer may not be able to take the lead as in the past; he or she may need more guidance and direction and even seem to be less sensitive and thoughtful. Nevertheless, maintaining this aspect of the relationship may be a vital expression of togetherness, and a valuable way of releasing tension for both partners. So much may seem to have changed—the sexual act itself, the degree of interest shown by the sufferer; but this may simply be due to the particular way the disease affected him or her; or it may be a sign of depression, or a side-effect of certain forms of medication. It may be necessary to shift the focus away from the sexual act towards other physical ways of communicating affection and warmth—cuddles, hugs, stroking, massaging.

As discussed in Chapter 3, there are situations where the changes in the relationship have been so great that the sexual area seems empty and meaningless. This may be the case if the problems early on were attributed to your partner being difficult or awkward and not to the onset of the disease. Sorting out your own needs for love and affection in the midst of this may well require outside help from a good counselling service.

Safety

It is well known that most accidents occur in the home, and in most homes it is possible to identify a number of potential dangers; not all risks can be removed or foreseen, but it is well worth dealing with the more obvious ones.

Dangerous substances—medicines, cleaning fluids, weed-killers and the like—should be clearly labelled and preferably locked away. Some carers have found 'child-proof' locks and catches quite helpful in this respect. These can be fitted to cupboard doors, making them difficult to open in the usual way, but fairly easy to open if you know how.

Fire is a major risk: open fires should be guarded (including coal-effect gas fires on which the sufferer may throw paper as if it were a real fire!). Gas appliances fitted with pilot lights are probably safer than those where the person has to ignite the gas; but all gas appliances should be regularly serviced to ensure they are operating efficiently. If the person smokes, this will need to be monitored and supervised. Some sufferers seem to forget about smoking; others want more and more, losing the ability to space out the cigarettes during the day. The routine of completely stubbing out cigarettes in an ashtray should be encouraged and emphasised. Make sure the sufferer's favourite armchair is made of fire-resistant materials —some of the older foam-filled chairs take only a moment's carelessness with a lighted cigarette to ignite into a blazing inferno of flames, smoke and fumes. If there is a fire-risk arising from the sufferer's loss of skill, matches and lighters should be kept by the carer, ensuring that smoking is always supervised. It may be worth considering the possibility of installing smoke detectors now that they are widely available, together with a fire extinguisher or fire blanket to put out any fire that may be detected.

Boiling water is another potential hazard, and sufferers may need particular supervision in the kitchen if their judgement seems impaired. Electric kettles with automatic cut-outs to prevent them boiling dry are a sensible precaution.

Some carers use locked doors as a way of preventing the person wandering off and getting lost, and in some circumstances this can be a sensible precaution. Remember, however, that internal locks can also be a hazard—the person may lock the bathroom door and not be able to open it again. Some form of lock is essential for your own privacy, of course; perhaps the best compromise is a simple to use (and not too strong) bolt.

Falls are especially dangerous in older people with brittle bones that fracture easily and mend slowly. Firmly fixed carpets are safer than loose rugs; remove any loose or trailing cables; make sure handrails are adequate on staircases; keep the floor clear of anything the person could trip over; make sure any furniture the person holds onto in order to get around is solid and stable. If the person does have a fall, and you are unable to get them up again, many carers have found that the local police or ambulance service can be very helpful. If you need to lift the person often, check with the district nurse or physiotherapist that you are using the method that does least damage to your back.

Medication and health

There are at present no medications of proven effectiveness in reversing or even slowing down the process of AD. Most of the medicines and tablets prescribed for the sufferer will be for other physical conditions. Or they will have been prescribed in an attempt to reduce some of the AD-related problems—by improving sleep, reducing restlessness and agitation, improving mood or whatever. Try to develop a good relationship with the prescribing doctor. Ask him what each item of medication is for, and what its effects are likely to be. Many doctors do not volunteer full explanations to carers, but, if asked, you will find them more forthcoming. Don't be afraid to ask questions; remember, the doctor finds it difficult to gauge how much to explain to each person. Some medications are available in different forms, so if you are finding the sufferer is not able to swallow the pills prescribed, it is worth asking whether a liquid or syrup form is available. Similarly, check when and how often the medication should be given; with some it is important that the dose is well spaced out; with others it could all be given at once with the same effects. As far as sleeping tablets and medication to reduce agitation are concerned, the time at which it is given can make all the difference between a good night's sleep and being awoken at 4 a.m.

Your doctor will not have all the answers, of course, but he can provide invaluable guidance. One of the problems is that a particular drug may have a good effect on one patient and none on another who is similar. Generally speaking, the effects of drugs on older people are much more variable, and so it becomes quite difficult to predict how an individual will respond. Prescribing then contains an element of trial and error. Your doctor will need feedback from you, the carer, so that the drug and its dosage can be adjusted to suit the needs of the individual sufferer. In the case of drugs to reduce agitation, a balance has to be achieved between having too little effect to be useful, and over-sedating the person to the point where he or she becomes more confused, sleeping most of the time and having trouble even with walking. Don't despair if new medication doesn't help immediately. Keep in close touch with the doctor, and follow his advice on adjusting the dose and its timing to achieve the best results. Most carers rightly realise that drugs are potentially dangerous substances to be used with great care. It is unwise, however, to change doses or stop a particular medication without consulting the doctor concerned. You could, without knowing it, stop a drug vital to the sufferer's physical well-being. If several doctors are prescribing medication for the sufferer, make sure each knows what the other is giving, as some drugs should not be given together. It could be worth making a list of what you actually give the sufferer each day.

Safety of drugs is important; unused supplies should be thrown away and the current medicines locked in a cupboard. If the sufferer lives alone, it is unlikely that he or she will be capable of managing medication unaided. Preferably, someone else should look after the medication and give it to the sufferer at the appropriate times—a neighbour, friend or family member living nearby might do this. At most, one day's supply should be left out, marked with clear directions, and all other medications locked away. It is surprising how often AD sufferers living alone are expected to take responsibility for complex regimes of medication by doctors who are merely responding to the person's physical condition and do not take the person's overall capabilities into account. One of the major causes of AD sufferers having additional confusion is the effects of medication taken inappropriately; so it is vital to get this area right if the sufferer is to survive alone at home.

It can be difficult at times to persuade the sufferer to take the medication; perhaps he or she is unable to see any need for it. Sometimes it is a large pill which is difficult to swallow or a foul tasting liquid that causes the problem. Try asking for it in another form. Some medication may be taken with a drink; in dire circumstances, some carers have disguised liquids in a drink or crushed tablets and mixed them with jam. Before taking such steps you should check with the doctor that such procedures are advisable, and that the medication is important enough to justify such desperate measures. It is worth being firm over medication for restlessness and agitation because once it begins to work the person should become more amenable and co-operative anyway. If confrontations continue indefinitely, you really should ask your doctor whether it is worthwhile, and perhaps consider enlisting the help of someone from outside, such as a community nurse.

One of the concerns carers have about some homes is that medication is used over zealously to render the person more manageable, reducing him to the condition of a 'zombie'; the person's speech becomes slurred; he seems about to fall asleep at any moment. The drugs in use are usually the so-called 'major tranquillizers': chlorpromazine ('Largactil'), thioridazine ('Melleril') and haloperidol ('Serenace'). In psychiatry, these drugs are used most often to control the symptoms of schizophrenia, which they have achieved with great success. In AD their use is aimed at reducing the person's level of internal distress, agitation, and restlessness. Sometimes it is difficult to see where the dividing line between treating the sufferer's symptoms and making life easier for the carers should be drawn. Restlessness, aggression and agitation are difficult to manage for the carers, and are undoubtedly potentially distressing for the sufferer. However, this does lead to suggestions that these drugs are being used 'just' to make life easier for the staff of the home or the family. ,The important thing to remember is that they are powerful drugs, with many side-effects. If they are being used, it should be under close medical supervision, preferably by a psychiatrist who is the specialist with most experience of them. The minimum dose possible should be given, and it should be regularly reviewed and reduced if the person shows signs of over-sedation. A watch must be kept for the person becoming rigid and stiff, or developing a tremor like that seen in Parkinson's Disease together with difficulties in walking. If the dose cannot be reduced without the person's problems surfacing again, additional medication may be necessary, similar to that used in Parkinson's Disease. Efforts are being made to find more effective alternatives to these major tranquillizers, but in the meantime their use is justifiable—with care, caution and good medical supervision.

Clearly, a good relationship with a doctor is of the utmost importance if medication is to be managed well. The same applies to the person's general health. Regular check-ups are advisable. Remember that the sufferer may not be able to describe his symptoms clearly. If there is a sudden change in the person's condition, there may be a physical problem—urine infections, chest infections and constipation are the most common! Unfortunately, AD sufferers are open to the same range of physical problems as anyone else, so it is important to ensure a check is kept on the person's physical condition.

When AD is very advanced, the person may suffer from occasional fits. Most of us have little experience of this; we feel anxious and unsure what to do when the person suddenly starts shaking uncontrollably; he may even lose consciousness altogether. The main thing to remember is to help the person fall gently and safely to the ground, or into a soft chair, so that no sharp or hard objects are in the way. Allow the fit to run its course, and when the movements have stopped, check that the person is still breathing. If the tongue has been swallowed, preventing breathing, lift the chin up gently and push the forehead back to clear the air passage. Above all, don't try to move the person from the floor. If it is the first fit, it is worth calling for medical advice, but this will probably not be necessary on future occasions. Fits are caused by a sudden outburst of electrical energy in the brain arising from damaged brain cells. Medication to damp this down is available. It is widely used for people who suffer from epilepsy, but in severe AD cases its benefits may be limited.

Alcohol

If the sufferer previously enjoyed a drink at the pub or in company, it is probably all right to continue—unless there are specific reasons to the contrary. The person's drinking may need to be supervised to ensure that consumption does not become excessive—the person will not be able to remember how many drinks he or she has had in the course of the evening. It has often been said that a little alcohol assists sleep, and it may be a preferable alternative to medication in some cases.

The main reasons for avoiding alcohol would be if it interacts with the sufferer's medication (check with the prescribing doctor); if the person has a form of dementia where alcohol has been a major cause of the problems—in such cases avoidance of alcohol is vital to prevent further deterioration and, in some cases, even to allow some recovery; finally, some AD sufferers seem to be more sensitive to alcohol, becoming less inhibited and even more confused by a relatively small amount.

Where you suspect the sufferer is partaking of the alcohol in the drinks cabinet at home when no one is looking, you can either lock the cupboard or, if this would cause a major conflict, water down the whisky (or whatever is the preferred tipple) so that its effects are diminished!

Death

Many carers see death as the final release for the sufferer from this tragic condition. It is of course hard to predict when this release will come; average figures of life expectancy mask huge individual differences. It is wise to be prepared; to have on hand details of an undertaker with a good reputation; to decide beforehand whether cremation or burial is preferable; to have discussed with your doctors the possibility of an autopsy— should the person's brain be used to further the research described in Chapter 8? Such an autopsy need not disfigure the person's body in any way, and will not interfere with your own quiet farewells to the person you cared for.

A dignified death, preferably at home, is what many of us

now aspire to; there is much to be said for the person remaining where he or she has been living—at home or in hospital—at the end, amongst people who know the sufferer well. In recent years, hospices have pioneered this concept of a dignified, personal death; as yet few have taken on any AD sufferers, but this may become possible in years to come. Euthanasia is illegal in most countries; but the consensus seems to be that medical intervention in the final stages should be limited to the relief of pain and acute discomfort. Should an AD sufferer with a chest infection be given antibiotics, which might prolong the person's life? If you have a strong view on this, one way or another, be sure to raise the matter with the doctors concerned. In fact, these life and death decisions often turn out to be irrelevant; I have known a number of sufferers who pulled through a chest infection perfectly well without medication! The important point is whether we should allow nature to take its course or seek to preserve the person's life at all costs. Each intervention has to be judged ultimately on the quality of life it will allow the sufferer.

Finance

Caring for someone who suffers from AD is costly, in terms of money as well as in other ways. This may be obvious: perhaps you have given up a good job because of the demands of being a carer. Other costs may be more hidden—the extra heating from having the person at home all day; the extra money spent on clothes to replace those that were ruined by incontinence or 'lost' during the person's last admission to hospital for respite care. It makes good sense to ensure that you are receiving all the financial help that is available. Increasingly it is possible (or necessary) to pay directly for additional services; this has the advantage of putting you more firmly in control of the service received, but can at times feel like a lot of responsibility. Getting all the financial help you are entitled to puts you in a stronger position to buy in extra help and aids—things that can make such a difference.

As well as ensuring you receive all the benefits and allowances to which you may be entitled, it is important that the financial affairs of the sufferer are taken care of adequately.

This is all the more important if the person's assets are substantial—they may include ownership or part-ownership of a house, for example. The issue here is that at some point the AD sufferer becomes unable to manage his or her own affairs. In order to protect such people, who might otherwise be vulnerable to exploitation, special procedures have been established. In England, this comes under the jurisdiction of the Court of Protection. When the amount of money involved is small, the Court can give permission for a relative or friend to manage the person's affairs. For larger amounts the Court appoints a receiver, who must regularly account to the Court for the way in which the person's affairs are managed. The receiver may be a relative, a solicitor, a friend or perhaps someone from the local authority. The Court makes a charge for overseeing this arrangement. It is generally agreed that this is a cumbersome and at times complicated and costly process. If the person were only physically incapacitated, he or she could give you 'Power of Attorney' so that you could manage the person's affairs. However, this cannot be used if the person is incapacitated mentally. Recently, the concept of 'Enduring Power of Attorney' has been introduced. This enables a person to choose someone to manage his or her affairs if he or she should become mentally incapacitated in the future. It can only be completed whilst the person is mentally competent. Your local citizen's advice bureau, a legal advice centre or a high-street solicitor will be able to advise on which of these procedures seems most appropriate. In due course, making an Enduring Power of Attorney may come to resemble the making of a will—something nobody really wants to think about, but an excellent way of forestalling future problems for those you care about. In Scotland and certain other countries different legal procedures are applicable, and it is wise to obtain local advice. Planning ahead is sensible in relation to these procedures because they can be lengthy. The more you can arrange whilst the person still has an overall grasp of his or her finances the better. Some sufferers find losing control of this area of their life very threatening, and if this is the case it is important to be tactful and sensitive, involving the person as much as possible.

Many everyday financial matters can be resolved without

resorting to such complex procedures. If the person receives a pension from the state or one of the various benefits, it is relatively straightforward to become an 'appointee'. This enables you to collect the pension or benefit, and so settle some of the everyday bills. Ask at your local social security office about this.

In the UK, some financial help is available from the government. Compared with the cost of care for the AD sufferer in a hospital or home, these benefits are pitifully small. Like any state benefit, there are procedures to be followed and rules to satisfy before they can be granted. Nevertheless they are well worth claiming because they will give you, the carer, a little more scope for buying in extra help—or even the basic necessities of life. The citizen's advice bureau should be able to tell you what benefits you may be entitled to; if not they will put you in touch with a welfare rights adviser who can. If you have a social worker, he or she will also be able to help. Often the procedures and forms are complex, so it's worth having someone who is knowledgeable to guide you. There are helpful publications available (see especially the *Disability Rights Handbook*—see appendix), but most of us need personal help to find our way through the maze of benefit regulations. Don't be put off—if you are determined you will receive your entitlement eventually! There are three benefits that are of particular relevance:

1 The Attendance Allowance

This is the basic benefit for a disabled person who is receiving care and attention at home, and virtually every AD sufferer should be entitled to it. It is paid irrespective of what other resources you have, and it is not taxable. It does not depend on you or the sufferer having paid national insurance contributions. You do not have to live with the person; the allowance is payable to any disabled person who needs a lot of help and supervision, whether or not there is a carer. If, for example, a sufferer was being looked after by two daughters, living separately but close-by, the sufferer could well be entitled to the attendance allowance. It could be collected by whichever daughter was the person's appointee and used towards the sufferer's care.

There are two rates of allowance, one where the person only requires day-time help and supervision, and a higher rate where night-time help is also necessary. It may take persistence to obtain the allowance. The first step is to obtain the leaflet (with form attached) from your local social security office—or see appendix for other sources. After sending off the form, there is likely to be some delay before anything seems to happen. Eventually, a doctor will be sent to assess how much help the person requires. With a physically disabled person, the assessor can ascertain relatively easily the level of help needed. An AD sufferer may, however, give a completely misleading impression, appearing alert and capable during the doctor's relatively brief visit. You need to make sure that you have an opportunity to speak to the assessor alone so that a clear picture of the problems emerges. It would be helpful to keep a written record for a couple of weeks of how much help and supervision—day and night—the person has needed.

If, despite this, you are turned down, or only awarded the lower level when you are giving regular night-time help, appeal immediately. Many such refusals are reversed on appeal. Back up the appeal with reports from your GP or other professionals who know the sufferer well. Give full details of the care and attention the sufferer is receiving. Eventually your persistence will be rewarded!

2   Invalid care allowance

This is a benefit for carers up to retirement age (60 for women, 65 for men). The carer has to spend at least 35 hours a week looking after the sufferer, who must firstly receive the Attendance Allowance. Again, you do not have to live with the sufferer to be eligible (or even be related). The allowance is taxable and eligibility is not so straightforward as for the Attendance Allowance, but it is worth seeking advice (from your citizen's advice bureau or welfare rights adviser) about your own situation. Again, the appropriate leaflet and form are obtainable from your local social security office.

3 Mobility Allowance

This benefit is for people of 65 and under who cannot walk or are virtually unable to walk. It is not taxable or affected by other resources and benefits. A medical examination is used to determine the extent of the person's mobility problem. Only a few of the younger AD sufferers are likely to be eligible—the rules do not cover mobility difficulties arising from mental rather than physical problems. If the person is able to walk a short distance—even if he gets lost very easily or doesn't walk in the direction desired—the allowance would probably not be granted.

Finally, you should bear in mind that some charities are able to offer financial help in certain circumstances. They are more likely to give one-off grants for specific purposes where help cannot be obtained from other sources. For instance, the Alzheimer's Disease Society has a Caring Fund that is able to make one-off grants to carers in certain circumstances—for a new washing machine, for example, if the previous one has broken down. If the sufferer was formerly in the Services, one of the organisations for ex-servicemen and women may be able to help; some firms have a welfare fund for long-serving employees; some trade-unions have schemes for their members. It is worth exploring these avenues if finances become a problem, or if you can see something that would be of use to you but is outside your financial resources.

Chapter Six

Coping with difficult behaviour

Aggression and abuse

If the sufferer becomes aggressive and abusive, lashing out at those who are trying to provide care, the carer is bound to feel hurt—emotionally at least—and probably rather confused. Why is it happening? he or she will wonder. Have I done something wrong or said the wrong thing? How should I react? Of course, if the person has always tended to be short-tempered or physically violent, it is easier to understand the current behaviour as an extension of the person's previous way of coping with difficulties. In recent years there has been an increasing awareness of how common violence is within the family, and it would not be surprising if a person who previously showed violent tendencies reacted to the undoubted stresses and indignities of AD with anger and aggression. If the person was once calm, placid and even-tempered, it may be much harder to understand. In both cases it can be very distressing and difficult to accept.

Why does someone become abusive or aggressive? A person who feels threatened or merely frightened will fight back in self-defence, especially if there seems to be no other way out. A person under pressure, frustrated at every turn, unable to cope with the demands being heaped on him or her, may explode in pent-up emotion. When the normal ways of expressing frustration, hurt and fear are taken away by this disease, aggression may seem to be the only way of expressing unhappiness and upset. When the normal social controls are stripped away, raw feelings are exposed. Diseases of the brain lead to fundamental communication problems. The person becomes unable to express feelings and emotions in the socially acceptable ways—usually guarded and controlled—that were learned in childhood and adolescence. The person may misinterpret the words and actions of others as posing a real personal threat, and may show the survival reflex of self-defence, as if fighting for life. Aggression may arise from any or all of three factors: loss of social control and judgement; loss of the ability to express negative feelings safely; loss of the ability to understand fully the actions and intentions of others. In the last case especially, the aggressor is actually very frightened indeed inside; such fear may give surprising strength and power—just like a primitive survival reflex.

Prevention is of course the best strategy for all concerned. To say that such incidents might be prevented is not to say that it is your fault if one does occur, but rather that the carer may be able to learn some of the triggers and danger signs so that they can be avoided in the future. You need to become aware of signs of increasing frustration and tension, the situations where the sufferer feels trapped or crowded, humiliated or undignified. Perhaps you should be wary of giving the person orders—make your requests more subtle and indirect instead. It may mean reducing the demands you are making on the person if he or she seems to be over-stressed by your requests.

Calming the person down is a good way of heading off trouble: give the person more space; leave the situation alone and return to it later if a confrontation seems to be developing. On your return, the situation may be quite different, the disagreement forgotten—at least by the sufferer. Remaining calm yourself in these situations is not easy—you may also feel frightened, angry and hurt. The sad fact is that your negative feelings may in many instances lead to a further increase in the sufferer's anger and aggression.

There are some exceptions to this rule of thumb, of course. Some carers have described how their own expression of annoyance or upset has struck home with the sufferer, who has then backed down. This is a risky strategy to adopt—an escalation of aggression could so easily develop. Much depends on your previous relationship and the sufferer's level of awareness. If you can, remain calm—by breathing slowly and deeply, counting to ten before reacting, saying to yourself 'It's the illness, not the sufferer's fault'. Leave yourself a safe way out of the situation so that you don't have to 'win the battle' at any cost.

If these incidents occur at all regularly you need to seek help. Perhaps someone from outside may be able to persuade the sufferer to do things that he or she completely refuses to do for you. Often the anger and aggression are most frequently directed at those closest to the person. This is of course grossly unfair, but it does mean that calling someone else in when the person proves unco-operative may break through that impasse.

You may also need someone who is prepared to listen to you when your feelings have been churned up by some instance of aggression. You need to wind down, deal with your own feelings; it is perhaps easy for the sufferer to forget, but not for you. Here your own network of friends or relatives can be useful; or you may find a professional who can give you some time to let off steam. You need to deal with your own feelings, allow them to subside, and not just bottle them up.

Apart from providing relief and emotional support, a professional may be able to help you work out what triggers off the person's anger; in some cases, a doctor may consider prescribing tranquillizing medication in an effort to keep the person's emotions on a more even keel. As discussed in Chapter 5, such medication needs to be carefully supervised and monitored to achieve the most beneficial effects. Ultimately, if the incidents cannot be prevented or controlled you may have to consider a permanent alternative placement for the sufferer.

Catastrophic reactions

The sufferer is suddenly gripped by upset and distress in the face of a failure or set-back; the distress, however, seems to be completely out of proportion to the severity of the triggering event. The distress may turn inward—the person may break down and sob uncontrollably in despair and anguish; or it may be turned outwards, erupting in rage and temper. Perhaps anyone under this degree of pressure would react in the same way, confronted with overwhelming demands, too many things to do at once and puzzling uncertainty. The sad fact is that for some AD sufferers, the unavoidable stresses of daily life may precipitate such a reaction. If such an incident has occurred you will need to ensure that stress and failure are kept to a minimum in the future and that any particular situations you know the sufferer will find difficult are avoided. Dealing with the catastrophic reaction when it occurs is similar to dealing with the bouts of anger and aggression described above. Removing the person, quietly, calmly, unhurriedly, from the source of stress is the first step. Reassure the person, saying perhaps that you realise how upset and unhappy he/she must be. Arguing with the person or reprimanding him or her will be counter-productive. However, be cautious in your offers of physical reassurance; your embrace or touch may be accepted as a physical sign of love, warmth and affection; but it may be misinterpreted as a further threat, crowding the person, leading to a further outburst of rage. If you feel this is likely to occur, use your tone of voice: speak softly and gently to the person, but allow him or her the space and time required to recover from the incident.

Depression and anxiety

It would not be surprising if the AD sufferer went through periods of depression and anxiety—there is plenty about which to be upset. Signs of depression include low spirits, withdrawing into oneself, an inability to enjoy food, activities or treats any longer; often crying, rarely smiling; the expression of negative thoughts, such as wanting to die or feeling hopeless and useless; unusual irritability. Anxiety may be shown by signs of tension and worry; an inability to relax or even sit still for a few minutes; appearing frightened or startled by the slightest unexpected noise.

It is sometimes difficult to pin down how the person is really feeling. There may be a lot of fluctuations, and the person will almost certainly have difficulty in expressing feelings clearly and consistently. Some of the general features of depression may occur in AD sufferers for other reasons—sleep disturbance, waking up early in the morning, loss of appetite, agitation, withdrawal. If the signs of depression or anxiety are persistently bothersome, and include many of the features described, a psychiatrist may wish to see whether a small dose of anti-depressant medication helps at all; or he may prescribe calming medication for someone who seems to be continually anxious and worried. In such cases it is very important for the carer to monitor the effects of the medication—it is very difficult for the psychiatrist to judge changes in a person's state from a brief interview with the sufferer.

Of course, some of the irritability or anxiety may be directly attributable to the person's own reaction to AD. When the sufferer is trying to express his or her feelings, listen quietly; don't try to push for explanations or argue with the person if she seems to have the facts wrong. If the person seems to be upset about someone who died years ago, sympathise with the person's feeling of loss first. If the person seems to be looking for something that has been mislaid, tell her that you too feel upset when you can't lay your hands on something important before joining the search! The feelings are real enough, but they are in danger of being ignored if they are wrapped in confusion, illogicality and misinformation. Acknowledging the person's feelings is an important step towards helping him come to terms with his unenviable situation. Remember too that the person may be responding to tension in the home or family even if he or she could not begin to put this into words. Ensure that you have opportunities to talk through your own feelings and their impact on family relationships—they can have an effect on the sufferer's mood as well as your own. Sometimes, being honest with the sufferer about your feelings can help clear the air—even if you know the sufferer will retain little of what you say.

One of the more puzzling features of some dementias (more usually MID than AD) is emotional lability. This means that the person's emotions are very close to the surface. He or she will suddenly start crying hysterically for no apparent reason; or laugh effusively at the slightest joke, again out of all proportion. Excessive crying can be quite hard to deal with at first because we are all so well programmed to associate tears with unhappiness. Once you realise that unhappiness alone may not be the cause it becomes easier to cope, by distracting the person, or not responding to the tears with the sympathy they would normally elicit. This difficulty in emotional control is a direct result of specific damage to the brain.

Wandering

This term encompasses several different and overlapping problems.

1   The person who is on the move all day long, never sitting down for more than a minute or two; she appears to possess boundless energy, but with no apparent direction.
2   The person who wants to be somewhere else, perhaps a place associated with the past—this is wandering with a purpose, although the purpose may be completely inappropriate to the time or place. He may want to go to the shops in the middle of the night, for example, or return to a house from which he moved 40 years ago.
3   The person seems to be looking for something or someone familiar, perhaps not clearly defined.

In each case, 'wandering' is being used in a physical sense—the term is not normally used for the 'wandering' of the mind that is so common in AD. Each type of wandering may need to be dealt with in a slightly different way. The ever-restless person may benefit from regular exercise or involvement in structured activity. Some sufferers are very easily distracted, and so may need a quiet, peaceful atmosphere at times like meal-times and bed-time when it is important for the person to feel settled. Some sufferers literally walk themselves into the ground, and may need medication to take the edge off their restless urgings. However, this needs to be carefully watched—sometimes the edge is taken off the person's mobility before the restlessness is reduced, leading to a great danger of falls and even the possibility of a fractured hip. Restlessness is very difficult to contain within the average home by a carer alone, and if this is a problem you would be well-advised to have regular relief—from a day-centre perhaps.

The purposeful wanderer can be very hard to deal with, especially if fit and mobile. One carer described how he left his wife alone for five minutes so that he could start cooking lunch in the kitchen. On his return, she had disappeared—only to be found 36 hours later, 30 miles away, still in her slippers. Needless to say, those 36 hours of uncertainty were harrowing for the husband and his family who joined the police in the search. There are some sensible precautions you can take, however.

Ensure that the person carries some means of identification. An engraved bracelet giving details of the wearer's identity and medical conditions, is ideal; name and address labels in the person's clothes or a card in the pocket may suffice. If the person is found, apparently lost, this will help you to be contacted as soon as possible. Make sure that your own address and telephone number are included, of course.

Have a recent photograph of the person available so that if a search-party is needed everyone has a clear idea of the sufferer's appearance.

Have a mortice-lock on entry and exit doors which can be locked with a key from the inside. This means that at night in particular, the sufferer cannot leave the house without you—you will have the key, of course! Some carers have reluctantly taken the decision to lock the person in the house whilst the carer is out to prevent the person wandering off. This should be regarded as a last resort and a potentially risky exercise; if it has to be done, at least ensure a neighbour has a key in the event of an emergency.

If you are unable to prevent the person leaving the house, try to accompany him or her as far as possible. Suggest some destination nearby from which you can both return home again.

If you discover the person has disappeared, inform the police, telling them of the person's dementia; let them have a description/photograph, details of what the sufferer was wearing and likely destinations (places where the sufferer has previously lived or worked, for example). Contact friends or family so you are not alone in your concern; make sure someone stays at the sufferer's home in case he or she returns—quite unaware of being the focus of a police search, of course! It is surprising how often sufferers do turn up at their own home, having walked miles; but quite unscathed, and just a little weary!

The third type of wandering, which involves the sufferer

searching for something or someone familiar, is a little easier to contain in that the person does not have such an overriding drive to go somewhere else. If within the home, it may be possible to distract the person into a more constructive activity, suggesting you both look for the missing article later. You may want to restrict access to some parts of the home—your own room especially—and this may be accepted with puzzlement, but not the anger of the purposeful wanderer who is frustrated by a locked door.

Toileting problems

Incontinence is perhaps the most humiliating of the problems that are common in AD sufferers, and it is one of the most unpleasant with which the carer will have to deal. It is not a problem with every AD sufferer, however; many retain bowel and bladder control most of the time, even as the disease progresses.

Remaining continent requires a number of skills—many children wet the bed at night even though they are dry by day. The same may be true for AD sufferers. The skills involved include: finding the toilet; recognising the toilet as such; dressing/undressing; planning ahead if opportunities to use a toilet are going to be limited; recognising the internal sensations that signal a visit to the toilet is required; 'holding on' until the toilet is reached; and the simple physical ability to walk to and from the toilet.

The length of this list indicates that there are many different ways in which the process can break down. Often it is in planning ahead that the sufferer experiences her first problems; perhaps she would benefit from gentle reminders to use the toilet every few hours. This has to be achieved tactfully, of course, or the reminder may be rejected as an insult to the person's self-esteem. So you might say, 'I'm just dishing up lunch—you've just got time to go to the toilet before it's ready'; or, 'We're going to be some time at the shops, you'd better go to the toilet before we go out.' As the person's abilities diminish, these reminders become increasingly important. If the person cannot walk very well, she may not have enough warning of the need to urinate to reach the lavatory in time. Two-hourly reminders during the day are sufficient for most people, although each individual's natural pattern needs to be taken into account.

Finding the toilet is more likely to be a problem in unfamiliar surroundings than at home. If the person moves to a new home, or goes somewhere else regularly, it is well worthwhile taking the trouble to teach her where the toilets are, and even provide signs to indicate their location. Night-times can be particularly difficult; in a strange house the sufferer may go into all the other bedrooms or even the wardrobe looking for the toilet. Try leaving some lights on to make the toilet easier to find.

Dressing problems can be helped by ensuring that trouser fastenings are not too fiddly (avoid buttons for example). Relatively few sufferers fail completely to recognise the toilet; many more have difficulties with some of the alternative receptacles provided (a commode disguised as a chair may not be recognised for what it really is). Some sufferers use whatever receptacle comes to hand—a waste-paper bin, a bucket, a sink. Sometimes a throw-back to previous patterns is evident—the person may get out of bed in the night and search underneath it for a chamber pot. Could a similar receptacle be used now?

When incontinence comes on suddenly, perhaps literally overnight, it is worth considering whether there is some physical factor involved. For instance, a urine infection may produce a sudden, urgent need to urinate frequently. This can be confirmed from a urine sample (which may look strong and even cloudy). Constipation can have a similar effect; it can also, paradoxically, lead to faecal incontinence. Your doctor will need to examine the person's bowel to check this. Effective physical treatments are of course available for both constipation and urine infections, which are the most treatable causes of incontinence.

As the disease progresses, a point may be reached where the person requires more and more help with toileting and becomes less and less able to express the need to go. Some carers become very skilled at learning the signs—restlessness perhaps, apparently looking for something, or even a certain look in the eye. Each family has its own words and expressions for the various functions involved, and the carer may be able to decipher what the person wants in a way that outsiders cannot. One of the most frustrating situations at this stage is where you have spent some time with the person on the toilet, trying to get them to perform, with no result. Five minutes later his or her clothes are saturated! Generally, this is not the sufferer simply being awkward! Feeling tense can actually prevent urination, as can pressure to perform (try producing a urine sample on demand!). It is important for the sufferer not to feel under pressure. Some may dislike you being so close to them; you may have to observe more discreetly; some may find that chatting helps distract attention from the task; others swear by running water as an excellent stimulus.

Incontinence at night is more common than by day. It is quite normal for older people to use the toilet once or more at night. If the sufferer is on effective sleeping medication, you may understandably be reluctant to wake him or her to use the toilet in case no one gets any further sleep. Toileting immediately before bed-time is therefore essential. If a person on sleeping medication wets the bed, a slightly smaller dose will sometimes allow him to be woken up by the urge to urinate, then go back to sleep again. You need to achieve the best possible balance between you, the carer, getting the good night's sleep you require, and having a wet bed in the morning. Sufferers vary in their attitude to a wet bed; some sleep undisturbed, others are woken by the discomfort. One of the reasons for wanting to prevent incontinence is the harmful effects of remaining in wet clothing—the damage to the skin which this can cause, for example. You may be advised to restrict the amount of fluid the person drinks. There is a kind of logic here—if little fluid goes in, little will come out, problem solved! Unfortunately, it is not as simple as that. Everybody needs a fair amount of fluid each day to remain healthy and prevent dehydration. Small amounts of fluid lead the bladder to shrink, leading to an even greater chance of incontinence. Whilst there is something to be said for much of the fluid being taken earlier in the day, there should be no attempt to reduce the overall amount of liquids given.

Dealing with incontinence is not easy. It's sensible to protect the furniture so that chairs and beds do not become soaked in urine, leading to a most unpleasant atmosphere! On the bed a waterproof mattress cover is essential; a plastic sheet across the vulnerable portion of the bed—over the bottom sheet, but covered by a half sheet across the bed—can often make changing the bed clothes easier to deal with and keep laundry to a minimum. Cushions of armchairs can similarly be protected. Try using a plastic bin-liner under a washable cushion cover. There are various pads available to absorb quantities of urine, removing it from direct contact with the sufferer's skin. These pads are disposable, which again reduces the laundry. Some are suitable for use on the bed; others fit inside the person's underwear, protecting the clothes. Many areas now have a nurse who specialises in dealing with incontinence, and a special laundry service to help with such items as wet and soiled sheets. If the sufferer is frequently incontinent, the delay of a week between visits from the service may make it less practicable.

If incontinence is very frequent, having a catheter fitted may be considered. This consists of a tube running from the person's bladder which collects urine in a bag, that can be emptied when required. Versions are available which allow the person full mobility, with the collection bag strapped to the person's leg. Whilst at first sight this may seem the ideal solution to incontinence of urine, there are disadvantages. Some AD sufferers find the catheter puzzling and uncomfortable and try to remove it; or the catheter may lead to frequent urine infections (which could make the person more confused); sometimes there is leakage around the catheter itself. You will certainly need regular nursing help if a catheter is fitted. Other urine collection devices are available which don't involve passing a tube into the bladder. The incontinence nurse will be able to advise on their suitability. Most are designed for the person with a physical incontinence problem who is mentally capable of understanding the device and its function.

It is important to prevent constipation; it can lead to incontinence of urine, faeces or both. Diet and exercise are important; with high fibre foods such as bran it is important to ensure the person drinks a fair amount; these kinds of foods absorb a lot of fluid. If the person uses the toilet independently, try to monitor how often he or she has a bowel movement so that you can judge whether constipation is developing. The sufferer will not remember! If there are problems with constipation, the person's doctor may prescribe medication to re-establish proper bowel action. Regular use of powerful laxatives is not usually recommended as bowel tone may be impaired. If there has been a build up, laxatives or enemas may be prescribed in the short-term. It is always worth seeking medical advice when faecal incontinence begins. There may be a physical cause.

Two problems that carers naturally find difficult are the person urinating in the wrong place (against a wall or in a waste-paper bin, for example) and smearing faeces on furniture, walls, etc. The first usually arises from the person being unable to find or identify the right receptacle. It can often be reduced if you are able to direct the person to the toilet or recognise the signs in the person's behaviour when he or she needs to urinate. Smearing often arises from constipation; the person feels blocked and tries to clear the block manually. The result is faeces everywhere. The person should be examined medically to see whether constipation is helping to cause the problem. It may simply be that the person is not cleaning up properly after using the toilet, and so the problem may be reduced by a little more supervision.

Accusations

Some AD sufferers become very suspicious, accusing people of stealing from them or of trying to harm them. Indeed, Alzheimer's historic first-case description was of a lady who believed someone wanted to kill her, and that her doctor was trying to assault her. When you are the focus of such accusations it makes it difficult to remain involved as a carer. If the accusations are directed at other people, you may be uncertain at first whether there is any truth in them. People's handbags do get stolen; people do get mugged. But would the home-help really steal the pension? Accusations make it difficult for workers, paid or voluntary, to come in and share the care; there is always the feeling that when accusations are made, some mud sticks, and complete trust is essential if outsiders are coming into a person's home to provide care and support. Your own uncertainty, which is natural if the sufferer has always been truthful in the past, also hinders the development of a good working relationship amongst the various carers involved.

The first step, then, is to identify the accusations as false—this is easier, in a way, if they are directed at you. You can then warn others of the possibility of such accusations being made so that they may be prepared for this eventuality. It is important not to go along with the accusations; but you could waste a lot of energy trying to persuade the person that he or she has got it wrong. Sometimes the accusations seem to be a way of making sense of what is happening: if the handbag is lost it must have been stolen and the home-help must have done it. That is an example of the kind of faulty logic involved. If you can pinpoint the initial concern, you may be able to respond helpfully. 'Your handbag is missing; let's see if we can find it.' It is often possible to respond to the person's distress without agreeing with the accusation: 'You must be very upset, everything seems to be going against you at the moment.' A sufferer who believes that people are against him may be very reluctant to take the medication that would calm him down . . .

As with other problems, it is important to blame the disease rather than the person and not to take what she says personally. Not all elderly people who are suspicious have AD; but if and when dementia is diagnosed the problems become a little easier to understand. Sometimes suspiciousness seems to arise from the person misinterpreting what is happening or being said to them. If the person is a little deaf, she may feel that people are talking or plotting against her. In such cases, ensuring that the person has an effective hearing aid (and wears it!), and taking trouble to ensure he or she is included in any conversation, can help a little.

A particularly difficult situation that occurs sometimes is when the sufferer accuses you of being someone else—an impostor pretending to be yourself! This can be quite disconcerting. We have mentioned elsewhere the carer who was not allowed into the bedroom by his own wife unless he was wearing his trilby hat. Sometimes the person may simply not recognise you any more; he may be comparing your present appearance with a memory picture of you 20 or more years ago. Your voice may help to remind the person who you are. At other times you may just have to leave the person for a few minutes in the hope that a different train of thought will develop. Looking at how you have both changed over the years in the family photograph album may help; but some sufferers will not be impressed by evidence that goes against their current beliefs. Their lack of recognition may involve interpretation of great subtlety—you've been very cleverly made up to look like yourself, but you're literally an impostor, posing as yourself. Fortunately, the sufferer can tell you're different . . . This is related to a feeling of unfamiliarity—the opposite of *déjà vu*. You look the same—but you're different in some odd, indefinable way.

Accusations can be very hurtful; as the disease progresses their frequency and intensity diminish, generally speaking. When you find yourself feeling hurt and upset, make sure you talk this over with an understanding person; to be rejected and perhaps no longer recognised by the person for whom you are trying to care is hard to accept. Sometimes it can be really embarrassing; one carer described how her mother called from the window to passers-by, asking them to get the police because she was being imprisoned. Fortunately, the neighbours understood the problems the carer was having with her mother. Having people around who understand and can support you is a tremendous help—it's worth explaining the situation to your neighbours, friends and any outside helpers before this sort of problem arises.

Hallucinations

This is where the person sees or hears something or someone that is not actually there. He may pick things up from the carpet when there is nothing there; or he may seem to be talking to someone when there is no one there. Often the experience is frightening and upsetting for the sufferer. One man saw strange people, some without arms, sitting in his living room; he angrily ordered them out, removing the cushions from the chairs so they would not be comfortable; then he tried to get his wife to help him drive them out. Another sufferer would suddenly look as if he were listening to something, then begin shouting, presumably at the person whose voice he had 'heard'.

It is important not to pretend that you see or hear the things the sufferer is experiencing; a few sufferers will accept that they're mistaken, but for many the experience is so powerful and real that they cannot believe they might be wrong. Again, it is possible to acknowledge the person's distress without pretending you are sharing their hallucinations. Reassure them that everything will be all right, that everything is under control. Show them that you are calm and not frightened.

Hallucinations arise from the damage to the person's brain. Some respond to treatment with tranquillizing drugs, so it's well worth seeking medical advice. The doctor will want to check there is no physical problem leading to an added mild delirium in which visual hallucinations may occur. Certain drugs and combinations of drugs may actually contribute to hallucinations in a damaged brain, so this will also need checking out. Sometimes hallucinations are associated with the person's problems in hearing or seeing, so it may also help to check that these are corrected by spectacles or a hearing aid as far as possible. For people with poor vision, some visual hallucinations may be based on a visual illusion, the person being unable to work out what is real from what is imagined.

Repetition and clinging

Unlike some of the problems previously mentioned, these can be tolerable in small doses. On the other hand, if they go on and on and on, the effect can resemble the torture of dripping water, eating away at the carer's reserves of patience, endurance and tolerance. The first twenty times the sufferer asks you the same question, you may be able to answer calmly, but before long the most saintly of us may begin to show signs of irritation. When the person follows you everywhere, always one pace behind, you will soon begin to cry out for some space to yourself. One carer described how her mother followed her everywhere, even banging on the toilet door to check she was still there.

These problems arise from the person's poor memory, together with a profound sense of insecurity. The sufferer is never really certain what is going on in his or her life, never really understands what is happening. There is this constant need for reassurance, which is sometimes so great that it seems to prevent the person hearing the reassurance when it is given. The person's memory problems make judging the passage of time incredibly difficult. If you are out of the room for five minutes, it may seem like an hour. An hour's absence may seem like a day. The person has to cling on to you so as not to feel bereft and entirely alone in this apparent ocean of time and space; as long as the carer can be seen, there is a point of safety; but perhaps it is one that cannot be relied upon to be there... always so it must be checked and re-checked to confirm that all is still safe.

The first and most important way of coping with repetition or clinging is to ensure that you do have plenty of time and space away from these demands by sharing the care with others. This will help the sufferer to become accustomed to you not always being there, and help him or her to give you more space as the care is shared. You need to have ways of escaping—a walk around the block, a neighbour you can pop into, your own (lockable) room—when the demands are getting on top of you. It is almost impossible to cope with these difficulties if you are tense and on edge. One carer described how her personal stereo with headphones enabled her to be physically with the sufferer but mentally miles away, immersed in her favourite music, thus making it very easy to relax and ignore the sufferer's repeated questions.

Another thing worth trying is writing down where you have gone and when you will be back. If the sufferer can read the time from the clock, this will help her to predict your return. Give yourself some leeway in case you are delayed—this system is only helpful if it is utterly reliable. If the same question comes up again and again, try writing the answer clearly on a piece of card or in the sufferer's note-book, and refer her to this when the question recurs. Try responding to the person's insecurity. Rather than answer the particular question again, tell the sufferer that all will be well, everything is in safe hands, all is taken care of. If there is a particularly irritating question and you feel strong, it may be worth simply ignoring the person and looking away whenever it is asked, whilst talking to them normally at other times. If the question never gets a response it may in time be asked less often.

Loss of inhibitions

Sometimes people with AD behave in a way that would have horrified them before the onset of the disease—removing clothes in front of other people or walking into a room with trousers round one's ankles. The person may touch their genitals in public; or behave in a physically provocative way to someone else.

There is little to be gained by reacting strongly to such behaviour. The person's loss of awareness and loss of social control arise from damage to the brain. Lead the person gently out of the room or point out that what he or she is doing is inappropriate. Often the action itself is not wrong, but it is in the wrong place, at the wrong time, or directed towards the wrong person. Sometimes there may be another reason for the behaviour; touching the genitals may indicate a need to go to the toilet; undressing may be due to tight, ill-fitting or uncomfortable clothes. The person may need something to occupy his hands. Many of us find socially acceptable ways of fidgeting—it's worth seeing if the sufferer can be encouraged to fiddle with something else—beads or some material perhaps.

A few sufferers start to use words that were not previously known to be part of the person's vocabulary! It can be very upsetting to see someone change so drastically, perhaps becoming quite foul-mouthed. Again, over-reacting is not helpful; the person may, however, benefit from feedback that such language is inappropriate. In cases where it seems that the person's speech consists almost entirely of expletives, this may be due to damage to the brain's language system. Swear words seem to be part of a separate system, one that may come into play when the normal language function is severely impaired. Try to encourage the person's efforts to communicate in other ways—through gesture and acceptable words and phrases.

Excessive noise

One of the most difficult problems is when the person shouts, screams, or generally creates a loud disturbance. One carer described how awful she felt when her mother screamed all night; knowing the walls of the flat were paper-thin, she imagined her neighbours must have thought she was murdering her mother. Sometimes the same word or phrase is repeated over and over again; perhaps the sufferer calls out for someone continuously, even when that person is by her side; sometimes the person will be fairly quiet until you try to get him or her to go to the toilet or undress for bed. Then the screaming and shouting beings...

If this is your problem, you should seek medical help urgently, probably from a psychiatric team. They will not necessarily have the answer, but they can try to rule out some of the possible causes, and ensure that you have the relief and support you will undoubtedly need. One common cause is that the person is actually in pain, the cause of which can sometimes be ascertained by a careful medical evaluation. The pain, if identified, may be alleviated with appropriate pain-killers. Another possible reason is that the person is very frightened or is hallucinating, shouting at people who aren't there. Both these may be tackled by medication. Sometimes for people who have severe hearing and eye-sight problems it almost seems like a way of creating some stimulation. Other forms of stimulation—touch (rubbing the person's back, for example) or favourite music played through headphones—may calm them down. If you live with a sufferer of this kind you will certainly need ear-plugs, and if nothing seems to reduce the amount of noise, you will need to consider very soon how viable it is to look after the person at home. Fortunately, this is a comparatively rare problem; it is certainly one of the most difficult to manage.

Chapter Seven

Getting the help you need

The first steps

In Britain, the family doctor or general practitioner (GP) is the key to gaining access to a number of services. In Chapter 1 the importance of a proper and thorough medical evaluation and diagnosis was emphasised. This needs to be arranged by your GP. If the GP refers you to a hospital specialist, this may open the way to other sources of help. The third major source of entry to the support services is the local authority social services department. However, it would be grossly misleading to suggest that all you need do is visit these professionals, after which a range of support services will be arranged for you. It is the experience of many carers that services are not offered— they have to be requested. Most professionals may not even be aware of the whole range of support services available in the locality. It often seems as if you can only have what you need if you already know what it is! But how can you *possibly* know if you are not aware of what is available? The answer to this impasse is to find someone knowledgeable about local resources and services; it must be local because there are differences between one part of a city and another, one town and the next. This person may be one of the professionals—a social worker or a GP, for example; or you may well find that other carers, ones who have already found their way through the maze of services, are able to give you most help. These people can be contacted through you local Alzheimer's Society group (see appendix for address of national body, which can give you local contacts).

Occasionally carers report that their GP or other professional is not very helpful, perhaps because their knowledge of the

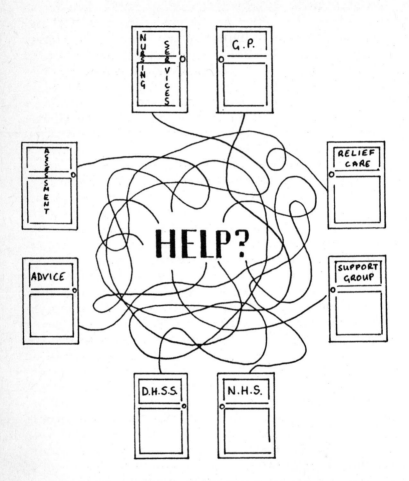

Fig. 4 Help is available – but finding it is hardly ever easy or straightforward

impact of AD is rather limited. Some GPs, for example, may not see the point of referring the patient to a hospital specialist on the grounds that nothing can be done for an AD sufferer. If you persist with your request, the GP may acquiesce and make the referral. If not, you could try seeing another doctor in the same practice who may have a different attitude; or in the last resort it is possible to change your GP. Other carers may be able to suggest an especially helpful GP; you will need to check whether he or she is prepared to take you on. If you can find a practical reason for the change (better surgery hours, more convenient location), this can avoid you being seen as a 'difficult' patient. The transfer can either be arranged between the two GPs involved, or if you prefer it, through the Family Practitioner Committee (the address will be on your medical card). The GP plays such an important role in the co-ordination of services for people living at home that it is worthwhile ensuring you are with the one who is right for you and the sufferer.

If, having been referred to a hospital specialist, you feel unhappy with the outcome of the various investigations and so on, you are entitled to ask for a second opinion from another hospital specialist, arranged by your GP. Increasingly, some of the major centres are offering a Memory Clinic, which offers a full diagnostic evaluation and helpful advice on future management. Some of these, (the Maudsley Hospital in London, for example) accept referrals from a wide area, although there may be a waiting-list. The Alzheimer's Society will be aware if there are such clinics in your area. If you are unhappy with the response from social services, ask to speak to the team manager about the problem; in the last resort, your elected councillor can look into the matter (name and address from the appropriate Town or County Hall).

In order to get some help organised, you will need to be persistent, aware of what is available, and conscious of the fact that you do have some limited choice and control in the matter—even if you are unfortunate enough to find that your first approaches prove unfruitful.

In the next section, some ways of obtaining relief from caring will be described; here we list some of the practical help that is fairly widely available.

a) Home-help: practical help with housework, cleaning, laundry, shopping, etc., for a certain number of hours per week; in some areas there is also help with personal care (Social Services).

b) Meals on wheels: a hot meal delivered to the home around midday on certain days of the week (arranged through Social Services).

c) Care attendant: someone who comes into the home and helps the sufferer with personal care—getting dressed, supervising meals, or almost anything else that meets the needs of the sufferer and/or the carer. (Some social services home helps have this broader remit; there are also voluntary agencies—Crossroads, for example—in some areas.)

d) District nurse: nursing care at home—bathing, getting up and going to bed, nursing procedures—changing dressings, etc.; advice on incontinence and aids; advice on correct lifting techniques (arranged through GP).

e) Continence adviser: advice on incontinence and useful aids, pads, etc; where there is not a continence adviser, the district nurse or health visitor will be able to advise on these matters (all arranged through GP).

f) Laundry service: in some areas this service will launder bed-linen, etc. where there is an incontinence problem (through Social Worker or GP).

g) Occupational therapist (OT): Advises on and arranges aids and adaptations at home—for example, bath seat and grab rail, specially adapted cutlery; aids to make dressing easier, etc. (arranged through Social Services or hospital specialist). Social Services may help finance more major adaptations (fitting a shower or a wheelchair ramp, etc). The OT will advise you on this.

h) Physiotherapist: advice on walking problems, lifting, walking aids, etc. (through GP or hospital specialist).

i) Wheelchairs, commodes etc: such equipment may be available from a variety of sources—through GP, district nurse or OT; or on loan from a voluntary agency (Red Cross and/or Age Concern are worth trying).

j) Chiropodist: foot care is important for mobility, but the skills of a chiropodist can be hard to obtain. In some areas, home visits are made; in others they are clinic-based; elsewhere there are few health-service chiropodists. Ask your GP for a referral.

k) Community Psychiatric Nurse (CPN): will make home visits, and can advise on coping with the difficult problems of AD, medication, etc. (through GP or hospital).

l) Health Visitor: in some areas, health visitors are mainly involved with child-care; elsewhere they are able to provide advice and support, and act as a link with your GP for families looking after someone with AD. The health visitor is an experienced nurse, although the practical side of nursing comes within the district nurses' remit. (Contact health visitor through your GP).

This list indicates that there may be a large number of services involved with any particular sufferer; exactly who and what is available varies from area to area, as does what each service offers. There is a growing trend for private agencies to provide help at home—both domestic and personal. Obviously your use of such agencies depends on the financial resources available to you. They are well worth considering if you have a special need that cannot be met by the other services, or if it makes all the difference between you giving up work or not. Social services or other carers may be able to give you a list of such private agencies. Voluntary agencies also provide some practical help, often helping to plug the gaps in provision within the locality. The local Alzheimer's Society branch will be aware of such services. This section has not included help from family and friends, which was discussed in Chapter 3. If you have a definite need that you think a friend or relative could meet, it's always worth asking. They may be quite happy to help, and simply not have realised that they could be useful to you. There's little to be lost if they do refuse.

Having people come into your home, or the sufferer's home if you live apart, can feel awkward at first. It's not unknown for people to spend hours cleaning the house in preparation for the home help's visit! Remember that these helpers' jobs depend on having people who need help; they aren't making judgements about you and your standards; they see all sorts of homes, in all sorts of conditions. Or perhaps you feel that it doesn't make sense to have someone come in and do something you're capable of doing. What you have to consider is whether you can use the time saved to do something else—perhaps have some time to yourself. You may feel you want to carry on on your own as long as possible. There is, however, much to be said for finding some sources of help early on; at a later stage it will be easier to increase the help, rather than start from scratch at a time when you may be feeling under pressure. It's also helpful for the sufferer to become used to other people being involved from an early stage.

Sometimes the sufferer's attitude can make it difficult to get help established, particularly if she lives alone. The sufferer, on the surface at least, may not see any need for assistance; he or she may even deny that there are any problems. 'There's no need for a home-help. I can manage perfectly well myself, thank you'; or, particularly galling, 'My daughter can do it for me'! It's important not to give up in such cases; try to introduce help on a basis acceptable to the sufferer. A home-help may not be acceptable, but someone popping in for a chat and a cup of tea might be. After a few weeks the visitor might wash a few dishes or bring in a little shopping, having passed the shops on the way. As the service becomes a familiar and established part of the routine, it may become acceptable. You may be able to appeal to the person's ability to offer something to the helper—someone may be seeking help with a project on the old days. Quite often it is the persistent, gradual approach that has paid off in the long run.

Unfortunately, not all services are flexible enough to offer help in this way; but there is a growing awareness that flexibility is required when offering practical help to AD sufferers and their carers. One carer has testified the usefulness of Crossroads, a voluntary organisation which provides paid care-attendants who come into the person's home: 'I don't know how I could have managed without Crossroads. The care-attendants came at the times I needed help, even in the evenings. It meant I could go to meetings at the church. They came one weekend when I wanted to go to a wedding. They helped me put mother to bed, and tried to fit into my way of doing things—they didn't tell me how I should be doing it.

One day they were due to take mother out for a walk, but I wasn't feeling well, so they did the washing instead. They were marvellous, they became just like good friends.'

Having a break

Some carers literally spend virtually every hour of day and night with the AD sufferer. There can be little doubt that this is tremendously draining and demanding, however warmly the carer feels for the sufferer. It is not possible to cope with some of the problems associated with AD if you do not have regular times to yourself away from the sufferer; times for refreshment, recovery and renewal; for maintaining your own interests and friendships. For some it is the only way of preserving one's sanity in the face of all those disturbed nights and days full of repetition and confusion. And yet whilst there is a strong need for regular breaks from the routine of caring, they need to be provided in ways that suit your circumstances. In this section some of the available options are discussed.

DAY CARE

This is probably the most common form of relief for carers of AD sufferers who live at home. The person is taken to a centre on certain days of the week. Lunch is provided, and the person is encouraged to join in activities and socialise with others. Health service day-care is provided in day-hospitals; the social services and other voluntary organisations provide day-centres. In a day-hospital there is usually some expectation that the person's condition will be assessed or some specific treatment offered, usually over a limited period of time. However, some day-hospitals do provide long-term support and relief. There are some centres that cater specifically for people with dementia (the centres run by the Alzheimer's Society, for example). In many social services day-centres, AD sufferers are cared for alongside physically disabled and lonely and isolated elderly people. Similarly, in day-hospitals sufferers will be attending alongside people with other physical or mental health problems (depending on whether it is a geriatric or a psychogeriatric day-hospital).

The foregoing indicates that provision is almost completely geared to the needs of older sufferers—with the exception of the Alzheimer's Society centres. These are being established in more and more towns in the UK, but they are still a relatively recent development, and can often offer only a limited service. Often younger sufferers are mixed with older people, which can be particularly difficult for the more aware young sufferer.

Leaving aside the lack of separate provision for younger sufferers, there is much debate amongst those planning and providing services as to whether it is better to mix older AD sufferers with other elderly people needing day-care. From the carer's point of view, day-care is needed that can cope with the whole range of problems seen in AD sufferers living at home. This means having a good ratio of helpers to clients; helpers who understand the problems of AD, and who are prepared to take the time and trouble necessary to communicate with the AD sufferer. It means a special eye being kept on the comings and goings of the AD sufferers so that they do not wander away from the day-centre and get lost; careful supervision of meals; and activities specially geared to the AD sufferers' abilities. Day-care that treats each person as an individual is what is required, with an atmosphere where the sufferer feels relaxed and as if at home. The good news is that many day-care centres catering for AD sufferers approach this quality; the bad news is that there still aren't enough places available.

However good the day-care, the whole system breaks down if there are problems in transporting the person to and from centre or hospital. This is probably the biggest single source of complaints regarding day-care. If you have a car and are able to drop off and pick up the person, there is no problem as long as the hours of day-care fit in with your own schedule (which is especially important if you're trying to hold down a job). Most sufferers are dependent on the day-care centre's own transport—usually a minibus or an ambulance service. These are notorious for their unpredictability and unreliability. The sufferer has to be ready by the earliest time the transport might call (say 9 a.m.) in order not to keep the transport waiting. It might not arrive, however, until, say, 11 a.m., depending on traffic conditions and how many other clients have been picked up on the way. The carer, having rushed to get the sufferer ready—breakfasted, toileted, hat and coat on—then has an agonising wait until the transport actually arrives. In some areas, transport may be cancelled without warning and without alternative arrangements being made—vehicles break down, drivers are off sick, etc. This makes a critical difference to the value of the service. If you had made plans for the day, they could be ruined; or your hopes of a quiet day to yourself may have been dashed. Efficient, reliable transport is a vital part of a good day-care system. The staff on the transport also need to be sympathetic to the problems of AD because the sufferer will spend a significant amount of time on the bus or in the ambulance. Some centres send a staff member as an escort, which provides useful continuity.

Centres vary in their hours of opening and how many days they can take a sufferer. Not enough of them offer even a basic 9 a.m.–5 p.m. service, which would begin to approach the needs of the average working carer. Most are open on weekdays only, and some are open only a few days each week. Others—particularly those attached to a residential facility— are more flexible. At one particular day-hospital, which also has an in-patient facility, sufferers may be dropped off as early as 7 a.m. and picked up during the evening, with the service being available seven days a week. This is, regrettably, the exception rather than the rule.

One of the benefits of day-care can be the regular contact with the staff there, who get to know both you and the sufferer. They can put you in touch with other forms of help and provide vital support by giving you an opportunity to discuss the care of the sufferer in which you and they now share. Experienced helpers at the centre can be a real boon because of their expertise in working with AD sufferers. Many centres organise regular meetings for relatives to get together. These can be helpful in introducing you to other people who really understand what you are experiencing , and in gaining information about local resources such as private agencies or homes offering respite care.

Before the person begins attending the centre, try and arrange to visit yourself so that you have a clear picture of the place, the staff and what the centre offers. Many centres will want to meet the sufferer before offering a place to assess the person's suitability for the centre. These visits are a good opportunity to begin getting to know the staff so that once the person is attending you can keep in touch about any worries or concerns—changes in the person's condition, for example. Remember that communication through the sufferer may be misleading; one carer was surprised to find on his first visit to the centre that a substantial lunch was served. His wife had returned home saying she had had nothing to eat, and was eating another full meal at home. No wonder she was putting on weight! If in doubt, get in touch with the centre. They will be happy to answer your questions, and will be glad of your knowledge of the sufferer. It will help them to get to know him or her as an individual.

Day-care in the UK tends to be relatively cheap; in day-hospitals it is usually free; in social services centres there may be a small charge for the meal and drinks; voluntary agencies may ask for a donation to assist with transport and other costs.

In country areas, distances may be prohibitive for day-centres to be established if the sufferer is not to spend all day travelling! A recent trend has been for day-care to be offered to a few sufferers in a person's home—by other carers or a paid worker. These initiatives are likely to develop further in the next few years.

RELIEF AT HOME AND SITTING SERVICES

Here someone provides care for the person in his own home whilst the carer has a break. The duration of relief can be from as little as an hour or so to several weeks, in the case of a live-in helper. Sitting services have not yet been organised to any great extent by health or social services, and most are arranged through voluntary or private agencies. Crossroads and some Alzheimer's Society branches can provide sitters for a few hours whilst the carer goes out, for example. The cost is usually minimal. You may be able to find a helper who can come for longer hours, even overnight, through a private agency, but the cost would be considerably greater. Naturally, weekends and nights tend to be the most expensive times. For longer periods, providing accommodation for the helper is part of the arrangement, so the size of the home becomes important.

Some carers have found people prepared to live in for a period of time through advertising in magazines, etc.

It is a good idea to build up the use of a sitting service gradually. This gives you chance to get to know the sitter, and gives them an opportunity to get to know the sufferer and his or her needs without being thrown in at the deep end. If at first the sufferer sees the sitter around while you are still there, there is a better chance he or she will be accepted. Can the sitter do all the things *you* normally do for the sufferer? Sitters may differ widely in their experience and qualifications; some may only be able to keep the sufferer company; others, perhaps those with a nursing background, will be able to give the sufferer a bath or help him or her get ready for bed. The sitter will appreciate written information, if possible, regarding what needs doing, what medication is to be given, relevant telephone numbers if various situations arise, etc.

You will want to feel that the sufferer is in good hands so that you can really enjoy your break. No one else, of course, can give care in the way that you do, and a sitter may have different ways of doing things. Sometimes a slightly different approach can be helpful. Sharing care does mean settling for less than the best at times; and yet for your best to be safeguarded you must have relief. You will want to satisfy yourself that relief care is always of an adequate quality. With private agencies or private arrangements, the onus falls on you to check that the person is caring and competent by observation and, especially where an agency is not involved, through taking up references. Where there is an agency involved, private or voluntary, take up any concerns you may have with them direct as they will be very keen to maintain a good-quality service. As you and the sufferer become accustomed to the service, you may think of ways of adapting it to be of even greater use to you. Discuss these matters with the sitter or the agency. They will fit in if they possibly can.

Having someone coming into the home is the least disruptive form of relief as far as the sufferer is concerned; he or she only has to get used to a single strange person, not a whole host of people, a different environment, and two ambulance journeys a day, as would be the case with relief through day-care, for example. It also has the advantage of being potentially available over a wider range of times and days than most day-care, allowing you much more choice about going out during your free time. However, if the home is also your home, staying there will not give you the break you require—even if you are doing things you enjoy around the house. For you there is the added disruption of having a stranger coming into and using your home. Although it is less confusing for the sufferer to have to get to know only one additional person at a time, this does mean that while you are out the sitter is alone with the sufferer, and cannot so easily call for help or advice as would be possible in day-care. A number of carers have described how the sitter (who may be in fact an ex-carer) has been a great source of support, helping the carer go out with peace of mind, and having time to talk over some of the problems of caring for the sufferer. For carers such as these, the advantages of relief care at home have proved far greater than the potential disadvantages.

For carers who must endure the strain of disturbed nights every night of the week, paying someone to come in even once in a while to enable them to get a good night's sleep may be a valuable investment—if resources allow.

RESIDENTIAL RELIEF CARE

If you are going on holiday, have a lot of sleep to catch up on, or need more than a day's relief, finding the person a place in a home or a hospital may be the only practical option. These breaks are often for two weeks, but they can be for a longer or a much shorter period—a weekend, or even just one night. Some carers are fortunate to have another family member who is prepared to take the sufferer whilst they have a break. Failing this, there are a number of other possibilities. Which is suitable depends partly on how much care and supervision the sufferer needs and, as ever, partly on what happens to be available locally. Some hospitals have a few beds reserved for respite care. If you are already in touch with the hospital team, they will advise you on this; if not, your GP can request that the sufferer be assessed for a relief admission. Some social services have short-stay units within some of their residential homes, or are prepared to take someone in for relief if there is a vacancy.

Your local social services office or social worker will advise on what is available locally. Some private homes offer a similar facility. In each case, whether it be a hospital or a home, the sufferer will have to 'fit' the particular requirements of the service; some will take only those who are continent or do not wander; others will take only the more severely disabled. Although this is understandable when one considers the facilities and differing levels of staffing, it can be very frustrating if the sufferer's particular problems seem to render him or her unsuitable for almost everywhere! (See appendix for details of brochures listing homes).

One of the problems that arises when there are no beds specifically set aside for relief care is that it is difficult to guarantee that one will be available at any particular time. This means you may not be sure until the last minute whether or not the sufferer will be taken in, which can be nerve-wracking if you have a holiday booked or a special event to attend. Another problem that many carers describe is that the person deteriorates whilst in relief care. This may be because of the change of environment, the upset to the person's routine, and the inevitable problems arising from having unfamiliar care-givers. The staff of the home or ward simply do not know the person as well as you do, and are not able to understand his or her needs in the way that you can. Inevitably, the sufferer will not receive one-to-one care; there will be other people for whom the care-staff will also be responsible. However, they do have the advantage of working in a team, of not being on permanent duty day and night, and of having experience of a number of people with problems similar to those of the sufferer. In some units, especially in hospitals, the person's health may receive a good check-up, or an opportunity may be taken to adjust the person's medication. Some sufferers really appreciate the chance to enjoy the company of other people. The potential benefits of relief care may therefore outweigh the disadvantages.

One result of a period of relief care on the carer himself can be enhanced awareness of the effect that full-time care is having on his or her life. That sudden taste of freedom can make you realise how much your life has been adversely affected. For some carers, this can mean a reluctance to see the period of relief coming to an end. Some hospitals and homes have found this such a problem that they insist carers sign a 'contract' to say that they will take the sufferer home again at the end of the agreed period.

When frequent breaks are needed, some units operate a policy where one bed is shared by several sufferers—in rotation, of course! The system might be four weeks at home, two weeks in hospital; or perhaps four weeks in, four weeks out depending on the needs of the situation. Such a system enables the unit to offer something very close to long-term care for more people, but for it not to break down it does again rely on the carer being able to take the person home when agreed. For those carers especially who do not see permanent care in a home or hospital as acceptable, this may prove a useful compromise. However, the stark, frequent contrast between, say, a month at home and a month in hospital is difficult for some carers and puzzling for some sufferers.

One option that has been explored for elderly people with a range of disabilities is what has been described as the 'granny fostering' scheme. This involves the elderly person going to stay with another family whilst the carer has a break. The 'foster family' are paid for this service, having been carefully selected for their suitability for the task. They also receive some training in what is involved. Such schemes are usually run by the social services. The scheme has the advantage of offering homely care, which is more likely to be on a one-to-one basis. It should be possible for the person to visit the home a few times before going to stay so that it is not too unfamiliar. Generally speaking, families will be able to cope better with sufferers who are fairly mildly impaired; incontinence, wandering, sleep disturbance, aggression and so on are going to be as difficult to deal with as they are for the carer without additional back-up and support. It is well worth enquiring whether there is such a scheme locally, but they are still fairly few in number.

The costs of a break vary according to the facility used. Obviously private care has to be paid for; but social services also make a charge, usually according to the person's means. It may be possible to receive help towards the cost of private care, especially if the person does not have much in the way of savings. Counsel and Care for the Elderly (see appendix) or your local citizen's advice bureau can give up-to-date advice on this. Health Service care in the UK is free. If finance is a problem there may be a charity that can help—perhaps one related to the person's previous job or the Alzheimer's Society in some instances. Again, Counsel and Care for the Elderly maintain contacts with many charities who may be able to help.

If you have the luxury of a choice of homes, deciding amongst them can be difficult. They will differ in so many ways, and perhaps none of them will really come up to the standard you had expected. In the next section points to look out for in selecting a home are discussed. In choosing a home for relief care, one that regularly takes in short-term residents may be better geared to the special problems that arise with a short stay. Some are better than others in helping the sufferer to feel he or she is also on holiday, which may be useful if the sufferer is aware that you are going away. If you have the option of the person going somewhere familiar (a place where he or she has previously been; a home attached to the day-centre the person attends; a hospital where the person is known to the staff), this will certainly be less confusing than a place which is new to the sufferer and where he or she is not known.

When taking the sufferer to the home or ward, allow sufficient time so that the person is as settled as possible before you have to leave. Make sure you have given all necessary information to the staff; that the sufferer has spending money for cigarettes, a hair-do or whatever; that valuables are recorded and kept safe; and that the staff are aware of any special dietary needs, medicines or allergies. The actual parting can be difficult. Do say goodbye to the person, and tell him or her clearly when you will be back. The person may forget, but the staff will be able to settle the person more easily if they can remind her of what you have said. Ask a member of staff to stay with the person as you leave to help the sufferer through the distress of parting and waving; and, if necessary, to distract the sufferer from making an attempt to follow you. Don't worry if the person is crying as you leave; keep walking away, determined to enjoy the break you need. Don't let the parting be drawn out by trying to console the person—leave that, and the sufferer's care, to the staff. More often than not, the person soon starts chatting to some of the other people and the distress passes.

When you have a break it is important to make the most of it. If you spend most of the time thinking and worrying about the sufferer, you will not feel refreshed at the end of it. If you spend hours each day travelling to visiting him you will end up as worn out as when the sufferer was at home. Remember that the break is for the sufferer's benefit as well as your own—the sufferer needs you to be fresh, calm and patient, not drained and exhausted. Going away is a good way of getting the situation out of your mind for a while; planning lots of interesting, absorbing things to do is another. You may just want to relax at home or use the time to reawaken some of your old interests; some of the things about which you're always saying, 'If only there was time I would...' Catch up with members of the family or old friends you've not had time for recently. Some carers may take real pleasure in decorating the house or working in the garden whilst the sufferer is away—but don't drive yourself too hard! If you decide not to go away, don't visit the sufferer every day! Once or twice a week is quite enough if you're meant to be having a break. By all means ring the hospital or home, but not every day. Don't spend the whole time thinking what it will be like when the person returns; rather, use the time to build up a store of good feelings that will help you cope in the difficult days ahead. Above all, do things! Visit places and people that will give you an inner glow of pleasure and satisfaction when you look back at them. If you find the sufferer keeps coming into your mind, make a conscious effort to say to yourself that the person is in safe hands and will be well looked after; and then deliberately think about something else or get involved in something that will absorb your thoughts. This mental relief is an important part of being refreshed by the break. For many carers it does not come readily. It may take effort and some struggling to achieve.

Time to move?

If the sufferer lives alone at home, the question will soon arise

of how long this state of affairs can continue. There are various options.
a) The sufferer could move to a more convenient home, closer to the family.
b) The sufferer could move into the carer's home (or vice versa)
c) The sufferer could move into more supportive housing.
d) The sufferer could enter a long-term residential facility.

Where the sufferer already lives with a carer, usually the only option under consideration is the possibility of long-term residential care—in a home or a hospital.

Moving house can be a very stressful event and with impaired learning ability it is even harder. It will take much longer for the AD sufferer to become familiar with the new surroundings. This means that there is always a strong case to be made for keeping the person in a familiar place, particularly if he or she has lived there for many years. If a move does take place, the person will need additional support over the period of transition when he is likely to feel even more confused than usual.

Sheltered housing is increasingly popular accommodation for elderly people. It is provided by various agencies: local authorities through their housing and social services departments; by voluntary groups and housing associations; and through private profit-making companies. It usually comprises a number of independent flatlets, with a warden on duty who can be contacted by a call-system. Many have communal facilities—a laundry or a lounge, for example. At first sight it may seem the ideal solution for the person who has been getting into difficulties living alone. The sufferer will retain her independence, but there will always be someone around to keep an eye on her. The presence of other people in the block will help to prevent feelings of loneliness and isolation. Unfortunately, many such moves by AD sufferers—even those in the early stages of the disease—have not proved successful. Apart from the confusion associated with the move, it is often the case that the amount of help and support which the warden is able to provide is strictly limited. Even in an emergency, the sufferer may not remember how to call the warden. In some sheltered housing units the residents do not make use of the communal facilities provided which means that loneliness is not necessarily overcome. So before deciding on such a move it is important to check exactly how much help, support and understanding would be forthcoming from the warden. In private schemes where residents buy their own flats, it is important to be clear what would happen if the person's condition worsened—would he or she be asked to leave? If so, would there be a financial loss? Would additional support be given? Another important consideration is that the sufferer's new neighbours may be intolerant of disturbances caused by the sufferer; they will probably be living in close proximity; they haven't had an opportunity to get to know the sufferer. We can often tolerate behaviour in a person we have known and respected for years that would be unacceptable in a new-comer. Sheltered housing is not then an ideal solution; in most cases it will be inappropriate unless the scheme offers or has access to more care and supervision than is normally available.

Having the sufferer come to live with you, or you going to live with the sufferer, also needs to be thought through carefully. Such a move must be carefully discussed with all the people involved—other members of your family, especially those already living with you. If you live alone it will be mainly your own life-style that is affected; otherwise, everyone in the household needs to be in favour of the sufferer moving in; if not there will be tension and resentment in the air from the outset. When making this decision you may be driven by very strong emotions—duty, pity, love, guilt, pressure from others—but you owe it to yourself to make a decision which recognises the practicalities of the situation as well as the strength of your own emotions. Do you really have enough room? The sufferer will need a separate bedroom—can this be achieved without someone else being forced to share? Will you be able to get enough help from family and friends as well as the various services so that you can carry on with those things in life that really matter to you—your work, your own children/grand-children, your interests, your own friends and social life? Do you and the sufferer get on well enough to cope with being under the same roof? If you are married, the same question must be asked of your partner's relationship with the sufferer; if they have never hit it off, it is going to be difficult for your partner even if he or she has promised to support you. Is your home suitable for dealing with the sufferer's problems? It could prove difficult, for instance, if the sufferer has difficulty in walking and your home has lots of stairs! Can your home be adapted? What will the sufferer lose by moving? A home, furniture and many of the possessions of a life-time perhaps; less tangibly, she will lose contact with friends, neighbours and relatives who live close by; and with familiar places and things. This can be a difficult decision. Actually living with a sufferer can be much more draining and distressing than one might imagine from less intense contact, where one can readily escape from the repeated questions, the unpredictable behaviour, and so on. At home you would probably have to shut yourself in your room! It is worth having a trial period of at least a few weeks so that you have a clear idea of the likely problems before the final decision is made to dispose of the person's previous home.

The final option—moving into long-term residential care— may arise for sufferers living with carers as well as those living alone. It is a particularly difficult decision to make because of the connotations of having the sufferer 'put away'. For many older sufferers the adamant determination *not* to go into a home is only too evident—despite apparent confusion about virtually everything else! Some of the hospitals that are used for long-term care may once have been the 'workhouse' or the 'asylum'. These will provoke strong negative reactions in sufferer and carer despite the transformation they may have undergone in the intervening years. In the face of all these negative emotions, and particularly the guilt that they may well elicit in the carer, it is again vital to think realistically about the available options.

The point at which this issue arises varies greatly. For the person living alone, the support and help available may break down much more quickly than if the sufferer is living with a carer. The problems—neglecting to eat or wandering and getting lost—may be a serious risk to the person's health and welfare especially if he will not accept help at home. The person may be a danger or a threat to others—leaving the gas on unlit or becoming abusive to the neighbours. When all the other ways of tackling these problems have been explored, admission to a residential home may be the only possible course of action. Some sufferers who have become rather frightened and lonely living at home may welcome a move that enables them to be with other people and feel safe and secure again. Others are fiercely independent, which may make the decision all the more difficult—a move could override the person's wishes.

When the sufferer lives with you, the problems that lead you to consider residential care may be quite different. You may simply feel that you cannot cope any longer; it may be the person's aggression, the incontinence, or the awful fact that he or she no longer seems to recognise you. People naturally vary a great deal in their ability to cope with and tolerate the consequences of this dreadful condition. For many it is perhaps the thought of the poor quality of the residential care available that leads them to postpone serious consideration of this issue. It is well worth talking about the facilities available to other carers who have already reached this point—often they are not nearly so awful as their reputation suggests! If you have some knowledge of the options available, you can make a much more informed decision. The other side of the coin may be to seek other ways of tackling the difficulties at home—bringing in extra help, getting more regular breaks and so on. The choice is not always between the current situation and residential care; there may be other ways of changing the situation without the person having to move, and many of these possibilities have been described in previous sections. Increasingly, care in the sufferer's own home is becoming available, including, at a cost, live-in helpers.

Although care in a home or a hospital may not be as bad as you might have imagined, it cannot compare with what you provide at home. The staff are catering for the needs of a number of residents; rarely if ever would there be a one-to-one ratio of carer to sufferer. The staff will not be so familiar with the sufferer's background, her likes and dislikes. The physical environment may be far from ideal. On the other hand, the staff will not be worn out and at the end of their tether—they go to their own homes at the end of the day and so have many more opportunities to relax and rest than a carer at home; they work as part of a team, and so are not caring alone; they do not suffer the distress of having seen the sufferer change from his or her old self; they may well have ready access to trained and experienced staff and medical facilities. Although the home may be far from ideal then, its assets may outweigh its disadvantages.

OPTIONS FOR LONG-TERM RESIDENTIAL CARE

There are a number of different agencies that provide long-term residential care. Exactly what is available varies from place to place, and the sort of problems and difficulties which would make a home or a hospital unlikely to accept the sufferer also vary greatly. Local knowledge is therefore invaluable.

In Britain long-term residential care may be provided through the Health Service, the social services or in private and voluntary homes. The Health Service care is almost entirely hospital-based, with care supervised by trained nurses. Each patient is under the medical care of a consultant and his or her team. Where there is major physical ill-health and perhaps an inability to walk, help may be provided in a ward under the care of a consultant geriatrician. This may be located in a geriatric or a general hospital. Where the person is more mobile, care is likely to be in a psychiatric ward, often in a large psychiatric hospital, under the supervision of a consultant psychogeriatrician. There are usually no specific provisions for younger sufferers—they may well be placed in a ward intended for elderly people. Hospital beds are in short supply, and hospitals will normally only consider patients who cannot be catered for by other forms of long-term care—due to aggression, frequent incontinence, severe agitation, etc. Many of the large psychiatric hospitals which provide this care are scheduled for closure in the next ten years or so, and there is a move to care for these sufferers in smaller units, closer to the sufferer's home, or to encourage homes to take patients with a greater level of disability than at present. Thus in some areas it may seem that hospital provision is almost non-existent, whereas in others it is a real option—although usually with a waiting list! There is no charge at present for Health Service care, although the person's benefits and state pension may well be affected. Admission to long-stay hospital beds is usually decided by the consultant and the team; if you are not already in touch with them, your family doctor can ask for an assessment of the sufferer's suitability for this provision.

Social services provide residential homes for the elderly (often described as Part III homes). In some areas, there are homes or parts of homes specifically for people suffering from dementia; in other areas, residents are mixed regardless of disability. There are often definite rules regarding the type of difficulty that is not acceptable in a resident coming into the home—although these are rarely actually spelt out. If these problems develop after the person becomes a resident, most homes are fairly tolerant and continue to look after the person once they have got to know him or her. There are charges for social services residential homes, which are based on the sufferer's financial assets and resources. An application to enter one of these homes is made through a social worker, who may be contacted at the local social services area office.

In Britain, there has been a massive increase over the last few years in the number of homes that are privately owned and managed. There are also a number run by voluntary bodies and charitable trusts that are not operated on a profit basis. As both are governed by the same rules they will be dealt with together. They fall into two major categories: residential (or 'rest') care homes and nursing homes. Nursing homes must have a qualified nurse on duty at all times; they are registered with, inspected and approved by the local health authority. Residential care homes may have qualified nurses on their staff, but are not required to do so. They are registered with the local authority social services department. In both cases registration is intended to ensure the home provides a reasonable standard of care and safety for the residents. At present, however, the number of inspectors tends to be rather small so that the homes are only monitored very occasionally. Some homes are registered as both nursing homes and residential homes, and have to meet the requirements of both registration authorities. Each home varies in the level of disability and disturbance it will feel able to manage. Nursing homes generally take people who are more physically disabled. A very few homes take pride in their ability to cope with dementia-related problems; others refuse to take any person with dementia. Finding a suitable home can be difficult. Professionals are not always keen to recommend a particular home, but they may give you details of several to visit so that you can make up your own mind. The registration officers at social services and the health authority may have lists of the homes in the area, although once again they cannot make recommendations. Some hospitals have a placements officer who may help you identify suitable homes. There are other organisations that provide lists of homes (see appendix). In the London area, Counsel and Care for the Elderly offers a valuable service, recommending homes according to the person's needs. Each home is visited on a regular basis and many carers have found this service most helpful.

Fees are payable direct to the home. They vary widely from home to home and between areas. The more care the person needs, the greater the fee is likely to be. Nursing home fees are generally greater than those for a residential home. However, private homes are no longer exclusively for the well-off. If the person has less than a certain level of savings and capital (currently £6000 including property), he or she may be eligible for financial help towards the fees of the home from the Department of Social Security (DSS). Counsel and Care for the Elderly produce an excellent fact-sheet giving the details of the scheme, which has enabled many people with limited means to enter private homes. Often there is a short-fall between the fees and the person's total income. If this is not too great, Counsel and Care for the Elderly are able to advise on how it may be met from charitable sources. It is worth mentioning that if the sufferer owns a house which is occupied by the sufferer's spouse or an elderly or disabled relative, it should not be counted as part of the sufferer's capital. Where the sufferer's fees are met from his or her own resources, it is worth remembering that the person will still be eligible for the Attendance Allowance, which can help reduce the drain on the person's finances a little.

CHOOSING A HOME

If the person goes into hospital or a social services home, there will probably be little or no choice as to which hospital ward or home the person enters. With a private home, by contrast, you may find yourself in a quandary weighing up the pros and cons of the various homes on your list. Choosing the home that will best meet the needs of your relative is not easy. You will need to spend some time in the home, having a look around, chatting to staff, getting an impression of the atmosphere and the quality of care. To do this you have to insist on staying longer than the time set aside for the usual guided tour by the person in charge, which will naturally emphasise the home's better aspects. If you are able, watch a meal being served; apart from the quality and quantity of food, you will see how staff go about their job; how they approach different residents; how they give each person the help he or she requires; whether residents are given enough time or not.

You will want to consider the following matters in weighing up the pros and cons of each home:

Location: Is it easy for you and the sufferer's other family and friends to get to so that the sufferer will not be cut off from the important people in his or her life? Is it close to facilities the person may be able to use—a park, shops, a pub, for example? Is it on a busy main road so that the sufferer will be in danger if he or she wanders off from the home?

Physical features: Is the home geared to the person's level of disability? For example, if the person cannot manage stairs, is there a lift? Are toilets close to the day-room? Are the bedrooms of a reasonable size—big enough for an armchair and other items of the sufferer's furniture? Will the sufferer have a single room? Does the home look well-maintained and clean (but not too clinical!)? Are there carpets and comfortable furniture? Is there a strong smell of urine? Are the day-rooms small and cosy? Is there a pleasant view from the windows? Is there a safe garden area where residents can walk freely? Is the home geared to a sufferer who may wander off? Is it easy to find your way around the home? Are there clear signs and notices to help?

Atmosphere: Did you feel welcomed when you arrived? Does the home seem 'homely'? Is there a feeling of warmth between staff and residents? Are residents spoken to with respect, without being patronised? Is the home well-structured and organised without being rigid in its routine—or is it chaotic

and disorganised? How are wetting accidents dealt with? Are
residents scolded or are they changed quietly and discreetly,
without fuss?

Staffing: Are there adequate staff? Is there enough qualified
nursing input for the sufferer's needs? Is there ready access to
medical help when needed? Other services like chiropody,
hairdressing and so on may also be important for many
sufferers. How many staff are on duty at night? Do the staff
have any training/knowledge/experience of AD? Do they
treat residents as individuals, recognising that each has
different needs, interests and abilities?

Activities: Homes are generally not buzzing with activity, but
good ones organise one or two sessions a day and have readily
available opportunities for more informal activities—for
example, cards, knitting, music, dancing, etc. Are there
activities that will be of interest to the sufferer? Some may like
to help make cakes, others to water plants. Are residents
encouraged and allowed to carry out any small tasks which
they may enjoy? Is there an organised programme of events,
outings, trips? Is there contact with local schools and
churches?

Visiting: Are there any restrictions on visiting? Are visitors
tolerated as a necessary nuisance or welcomed as important
people in the residents' lives? Are visitors confined to one part
of the home or is free access allowed? Do staff talk to visitors
about residents in front of the residents?

Of course, the perfect home that is ideal in all respects does
not exist; homes change when a new person in charge takes
over; the quality of food may be quite different with a new
cook. Ultimately, you have to select the home that seems to
meet the sufferer's needs best. If you have a short-list of two or
three homes that seem acceptable, it may be worth taking the
sufferer to visit for a few hours to get some idea of his feelings
about the places. There is no point in showing the person
around several homes and expecting him to make a choice from
memory. Nevertheless, some sufferers may be able to express
opinions when they are there. It is important to try to grasp
whether the sufferer's objections are specific to one particular
home or a general protest against the whole idea. If the sufferer

is adamantly against the idea, emphasise that the stay you have in mind is only testing the water. It is important to be honest with the sufferer. Tell her that she needs special help and care which you cannot give—not through the sufferer's own fault but because of her illness/disability/memory problems. This will be painful for both sufferer and carer, and it will help if you can discuss the matter with a sympathetic, supportive professional. If the sufferer has already had periods of relief care, the transition may be easier. The important thing is to get beyond the negative image of 'going into a home'. The reality will have its positive aspects as well.

THE MOVE INTO A HOME OR A HOSPITAL

When making the move, always accompany the sufferer. Help the person to unpack and arrange his or her possessions in the bedroom to make it feel homely and familiar. Make sure the home has any medication which the sufferer needs, and that it is aware of any other medical conditions. When the time comes to leave, ask one of the staff to stay with the sufferer, say a brief farewell—and then leave! You may both be hurt by the parting, but this is not the time to let these feelings cause you to doubt the wisdom of your decision. The early days of adjustment may be difficult; if the staff run into difficulties in the first day or two, try to encourage them to persist. After a few days the person usually becomes more settled. Don't feel you have to stay away during this time, although partings may still be difficult. Often the sufferer's tears are soon forgotten once the carer is out of sight and the sufferer's attention is diverted elsewhere. The sufferer's home should be retained for at least a month after the move so that a proper decision can be made once the person has had an opportunity to settle into the home. This will be a good opportunity to bring other belongings of the sufferer's choice into the home, according to the space available.

CARING FOR A SUFFERER IN A HOME OR HOSPITAL

Many relatives visit less often after the first few months; it can be discouraging to visit a person who may not even recognise you, or who may be upset when you leave—especially if the place is not very welcoming. At the same time, many relatives feel tremendous guilt about 'putting the person away'. If you can retain constructive contact, this will be really valuable to the sufferer. Bring in things to show the sufferer or take him out from time to time; if you have transport, car rides are often appreciated. When the sufferer is more disabled, it should be possible to join in the person's care if you wish, helping the person to eat and drink, or doing the person's hair, for example. Try to keep up contact with the staff; make sure you tell them the things you appreciate as well as the things that aren't quite right. It may well be that all mother's vests have disappeared; but the staff need to know that you value the care they have given as well. In a good home relatives can often strike up a valuable working relationship with the staff, getting involved in various events and activities. Relatives should be involved in and consulted about the care of the sufferer; and there should be a recognition of the carer's continuing concerns and feelings even though the pattern of care may now be very different.

No home is perfect. In some homes standards drop and unacceptable incidents occur from time to time. If you have serious concerns about the quality of care it may be difficult to voice them for fear of your relative being victimised. Yet someone has to speak out for the sake of all the residents. If the matter concerns a particular member of staff, you should see the person in charge; for more serious complaints, the Registration Officer may be contacted in the case of a private home. In hospitals there will be an official complaints procedure, initiated by writing to the hospital managers. Don't hesitate to act if you are not happy with the response of the nurse in charge of the ward or the medical consultant who is responsible for the sufferer's care. In a social services home, write to the director of social services at the social services Head Office, who will arrange for the complaint to be investigated. If you are not happy with the response, you may contact your local councillor who can look into the matter for you. Hopefully, you will not need to have recourse to these procedures, but it is important to be aware of the safeguards that exist. It is helpful to keep copies of any letters you send, and to keep notes of dates and times and the names of people involved in any incidents that give cause for concern.

The guilt that many relatives feel about the sufferer going into a home can be difficult to cope with. It helps to talk it over with other carers who have been in the same position. You must recognise that everyone has limits to their ability to care at home. By continuing to do as much as you can for the sufferer in his or her new home, you are at least contributing to an improvement in the sufferer's quality of life. It will mean facing the guilt each time you visit. If, on the other hand, you stay away, you will not be reminded so often, and you may avoid the guilt feelings—as long as you are able to put them out of your mind. People will tell you that you have no need to feel guilty. Logically speaking, they're probably correct. Many carers go to incredible lengths and make great sacrifices to avoid this situation. Unfortunately, this doesn't make the feelings of guilt go away. You are still faced with the unenviable task of choosing how to cope with them. The admission to residential care brings relief of many stresses and strains, but the impact of caring continues.

Chapter Eight

Is there hope for the future?

It is difficult to take much comfort from the future when you and the person you care for deeply are caught up in the clutches of AD *now*. There is no cure just around the corner, nothing that promises to change the lives of present-day sufferers dramatically. However, this chapter will demonstrate that there are signs that gradual progress *is* being made in many directions, to the potential benefit of the next generation of AD sufferers. It may also be of interest to know that in certain instances current sufferers and those who care for them can be involved in the quest for a greater understanding of the causes of AD, and in developing possible therapies.

The future directions to be described fall into two main areas: research into the nature, causes and treatments for the dementias; and developments in services and facilities available for dementia sufferers and their carers.

Research trends

Crystal-ball gazing is notoriously difficult in medical research. It is often said that some of the most important discoveries are made by accident, perhaps in the course of researching a completely different condition. It is nonsensical for anyone to say that we will have a cure for AD in five, ten or fifteen years—such predictions just cannot be made. But luck has to be worked at, and the realisation that a lucky break has just occurred may depend on years of groundwork and preparation, building up a thorough and detailed picture of the conditions involved. At the present time in the UK there *is* a considerable amount of research activity centred on AD. Distinguished researchers who have made a major contribution to the understanding of other disorders are joining the ranks of those with a long-standing interest in the dementias, and many young, gifted scientists are being attracted into the field. Research teams at the Universities of Glasgow, Cambridge, Bristol, Newcastle and Liverpool, at the Institutes of Neurology and Psychiatry in London, and at several of the London teaching hospitals, are among the most prominent. All would tell you it is not enough! Even more resources are being allocated to research into AD in the USA, and there is now a much greater sense of an international research effort devoted to this area.

Developments are often reported in the newspapers and on TV almost before they have been scrutinised by the scientific community. It is as well to treat these reports with a little caution—there is often many a slip between the excitement of discovery and its practical application to the problem. Sometimes media reports can be misleading. One day a news bulletin had the following snippet: 'Researchers have named aluminium—the metal from which many saucepans as well as many foil products are made—as being the probable cause of Alzheimer's Disease, the major form of senility.' That was the end of the news item! Suffice it to say that removing all aluminium pots and pans from the home (as one caring relative did) would be most unlikely to have any effect at all in preventing the onset of AD.

If you are concerned by any particular news report it is well worth contacting the Alzheimer's Disease Society—they have access to a panel of medical and scientific advisors who can evaluate the report for the benefit of carers.

Research on AD is at an exciting stage. In the 1960s, reports from Newcastle-upon-Tyne established an association between the quantity of plaques and tangles and the severity of the dementia; in the 1970s similar associations were reported between the severity of dementia and deficiencies in certain vital chemical substances in the brain. At the time both represented a major breakthrough in our understanding of AD. There are already several candidates for the 1980s, but only time will tell which is of most significance. Three of the most promising lines of enquiry will be discussed here. All have been made possible by general scientific developments enabling more sophisticated and detailed methods of observing the brain's structure and chemistry and genetic markers. Where Alzheimer himself had only an ordinary microscope with which to observe plaques and tangles, present-day researchers may have an electron microscope which provides a degree of magnification inconceivable to Alzheimer's generation. The difference is at least as great as that between examining the brain with the naked eye and using a conventional microscope. Similarly, there have been great advances in techniques for identifying complex chemical substances in miniscule amounts, and in the methods used to examine a person's genetic make-up. Of course, there is still a great deal that is not fully understood—the more we know, the more we realise how little we know!

As an example of this, we might consider the theory that AD could be caused by a 'slow virus'. We have all experienced a virus at one time or another—if only the flu virus. In this case, research has identified and described a form of virus whose action is much more subtle, taking a much longer period of time to become active. There have been suggestions that disorders such as multiple sclerosis may also be related to the working of a slow virus. Unfortunately, so little is understood of these slow viruses (or 'prions') and their mode of action that it is very difficult to assemble evidence for or against it. One might think that if AD were a viral disorder it would be infectious; that it would be possible to 'catch' AD from a sufferer. Here the findings are very clear: there is no evidence that AD can be transmitted from one person to another—unlike one rare form of dementia (Creutzfeldt-Jakob Disease) where transmission can take place, although not by everyday contact. Yet the knowledge we have of slow viruses is so partial that even this negative finding does not necessarily eliminate the theory.

The hunt for the AD gene

Several findings have led to an interest in pursuing the genetic, or inherited, basis of AD. Firstly, it has long been known that there is an increased risk of developing AD if a close relative has been an AD sufferer. Generally speaking, the increased risk is small, but it is quite evident when large enough samples of sufferers and their relatives are followed through carefully. Secondly, it has emerged that there are some families where the increased risk to relatives is much greater than average. Detailed family trees have been compiled and extensive detective work carried out to discover which members of the family developed some form of dementia, and whether this was likely to have been AD. This is quite an undertaking: some members of the family may have died young—killed in the war, for example—or suffered some other disease such as a stroke, which may obscure whether or not AD developed. Records are often inadequate; 20 or 30 years ago there was even less chance of AD being properly diagnosed than today. Problems were often kept hidden in the family or, as ever, put down to old age. Despite these difficulties, some families in which there is a very high family risk factor have been clearly identified.

The third line of evidence comes from an unexpected source. Down's Syndrome (mongolism) affects children from birth, in many cases leading to slower development of skills and intellect. Life-expectancy is reduced, and it has been noted that the brain often shows evidence of plaques and tangles—the Alzheimer changes—when examined after the person's death. Many (although probably not all) Down's sufferers show a form of dementia in their 40s and 50s. This can be hard to measure in view of the sufferers' low level of attainment. Many sufferers have spent their lives in institutions such as hospitals for the mentally handicapped, where the lack of stimulation has often been thought to contribute to the general deterioration as the years go by. However, a clear link between AD and Down's Syndrome has now been established. This is reinforced by the finding of a family link between the two disorders; that is, a relative of someone with AD is more likely to suffer from Down's Syndrome than the average person.

What is the significance of this link between two potentially disabling conditions? One of its most important aspects is that Down's Syndrome is known to be related to an abnormality in the person's chromosomes. These are the repository of the genetic coding system that has so much influence in making each of us an unique individual (apart from identical twins, who share the same genetic code!). This individuality is not located in one particular part of the body, but is actually found at the heart of every cell. Normally we each have a pair of 22 chromosomes (one of each from each parent), plus two sex-determining chromosomes; but in Down's Syndrome there is an extra one. This has been identified as a third chromosome added onto the 21st pair of chromosomes, and it is generally accepted that the genetic code for Down's Syndrome is located on this particular chromosome. The search for the gene related to the form of AD which has a strong family component has recently focused on chromosome 21 also, and there are now strong indications that it is located there. As if establishing the proximity between AD and Down's Syndome at this level were not enough, there was further excitement when it was realised that the genetic coding for the production of the protein 'amyloid' was also located nearby on chromosome 21. Amyloid has been identified as a major constituent of both plaques and tangles in the AD sufferer's brain. Could this then be the answer? Does the closeness of these three genetic codes explain the links that have been demonstrated?

At first, this seemed possible; perhaps the AD gene operated to give an over-production of amyloid, leading to its unwelcome appearance in brain cells in AD and Down's sufferers as they aged. However, other researchers are now saying this cannot be the whole story, as in some cases the AD gene appears outside the area of chromosome 21 known to be of the most significance for Down's; and the AD gene and the amyloid gene, although near each other, are not, it is said, sufficiently close for one to act directly on the other. Work in this area is proceeding very quickly thanks to the growing sophistication of techniques for examining genetic coding, and further progress will no doubt soon be reported.

There are, nevertheless, limitations to the work as it seems to be developing at present. Firstly, much of the research is focusing on cases of AD where there is a strong family inheritance. It will of course also be necessary to find what lies behind the many cases (probably the majority) where AD arises without a strong family history. There has been a suggestion that in such cases part of chromosome 21 is duplicated (as in Down's Syndrome), but several research groups have been unable to confirm this view. Secondly, it is not clear that locating the AD gene will necessarily lead to a basis for treatment. Many diseases are known to have a strong genetic basis—including heart disease, for instance. Yet whether or not the disease affects the individual with a genetic predisposition towards it can also be influenced by a number of other factors—smoking, diet, life-style and exercise in the case of heart disease, for example. As yet we know virtually nothing about which factors might have the influence to turn a genetic tendency to AD into a tragic reality. It may be that the genetic research will be able to identify something of the process by which the devastation of brain cells occurs in AD—as at first seemed possible with the link with the amyloid protein gene. This could lead to treatments aimed at interfering with these processes, or perhaps even a drug that could prevent plaques and tangles developing further. Finding the gene is then only a part of the story, important though it may be. It will probably not have such a profound effect as, say, identifying the gene for Huntington's Disease has had, because there is much less of a demand among relatives of AD sufferers for a test predicting whether or not they will in due course develop the disorder. In families where there is a strong tendency not only for it to be inherited, but to come on at an early age, this demand may develop. As experience is gained with the predictive test for Huntington's Disease, it may prove possible to ascertain just how helpful prior knowledge of such an eventuality can be, and—of equal importance—how accurate such a test can be.

Aluminium—the core of the problem?

We are familiar with the idea that various metals can be involved in brain-damaging conditions. Lead—from paint and petrol via car exhausts—is recognised as a major hazard to children's health, leading to problems in concentration and attention. The idea that the common-place metal aluminium might be related to dementia has been around for some time. Some evidence came from an unlikely source—patients who were regularly undergoing dialysis because their kidneys had ceased to operate effectively. It was noticed that a number of these patients developed a form of dementia, which seemed to be related to increased concentrations of aluminium in the person's body arising from the dialysis process. This led to the routine use of procedures to remove aluminium from the dialysis fluid. However, the form of dementia was not completely identical with AD—the neurofibrillary tangles present were not of the characteristic type. Similarly, experiments on animals showed the damaging effects of aluminium-based substances on brain cells, but without the specific Alzheimer changes occurring.

This lack of direct evidence for a connection between aluminium and AD led to the theory losing support. However, recent research into the make-up of the plaques in AD at Newcastle-upon-Tyne has established that at the very core of the plaque aluminium can be identified. Of great significance is the fact that it is combined with silicon, forming a compound that is very hard to dissolve. This means that it must have been present when the plaque began to be formed because it would have been virtually impossible for it to have moved there from outside afterwards. This combination of aluminium and silicon is also found in sand—although no one has yet suggested that AD is acquired by spending too long on a beach!

The crucial question regarding the presence of aluminium in the centre of the plaque is not how the metal was taken into the body, but rather how it passes into the brain, which normally has a highly effective barrier against it. This puzzle will need to be solved for a full understanding of AD to be gained. Once through the barrier, the possibility of aluminium having a role in the formation of plaques by disturbing protein production is quite conceivable, although the process may well be complex.

One possibility may be that some people are more vulnerable than others—their brains are more likely to allow the aluminium to act in this way, because of a genetic factor perhaps, or even as a result of the effects of a slow virus. Or it may be that imbalances in other metals allow aluminium to have a greater concentration than would otherwise be the case. Thus the problem would not be seen as a form of aluminium poisoning, but rather a deficiency in up-take of another vital metal. Calcium has been suggested as one suspect. It has chemical similarities to aluminium, and a number of older people do show calcium deficiencies, either through diet or from their body not absorbing the calcium from their food and drink efficiently. Interestingly, it has been reported that in some parts of the world (notably a Pacific island called Guam) where another form of dementia occurs with neurofibrillary tangles, the soil and water supplies have little calcium present, but are rich in aluminium. However, another toxin, found in local produce, is also under suspicion there.

The research activity that has been stimulated by the discovery of aluminium at the core of the plaque will no doubt soon begin to bear fruit by increasing our knowledge of the link between AD and aluminium. It is an area that could lead to sources of treatment perhaps involving efforts to balance out the person's disordered absorption of these metals through careful control of intake and exposure. Other metals, such as zinc, are also being studied, and the role of the pathways normally taken by iron is also under consideration as a possible route for aluminium to the brain cells. Clearly, AD is not a straightforward reaction to a particular environmental poison —the disease is both too wide-spread and too selective for that to be the case. The crux of the problem is why some people are affected and not others when there is such a wide exposure to aluminium and other related metals in the everyday environment.

A connection between levels of aluminium in an area's water supply and the prevalence of AD in that area has been suggested. However, to confirm this link scientifically would take a major research programme because regional differences in the prevalence of AD have not yet been established. Early reports may have over-stated the evidence for such a link, and until more positive evidence is forthcoming there is no reason to stop using tap water.

Replacing the lost chemicals

If we think of the brain as a complex telephone system, with messages being passed from one part to another at high speed, setting up a chain of commands for the simplest action, and increasingly complex networks of messages buzzing back and forth for more elaborate tasks, there must obviously be a very efficient means of passing messages from one part of the brain to another. In a telephone system, messages are transmitted along wires by electricity, or more recently by means of light along special fibres. In the brain, messages are passed by chemical means through a system of reversible chemical reactions. The chemical substances concerned are known as 'neurotransmitters'. A number of these substances have been identified, and some at least seem to be closely involved in the smooth operation of certain types of brain functions. For example, dopamine has been identified in the initiation and control of movement. It has been known for some time that there is a deficiency of this chemical in the brains of sufferers from Parkinson's Disease. This has led to the development of treatments aimed at compensating for the deficiency. This was a therapeutic breakthrough, and many Parkinson's patients treated with L-dopa were reported as having been in a sense liberated from the chains of Parkinsonism by which they had been confined and restricted. Subsequently other drugs, also thought able to act on the dopamine system, have been developed and used. It is now clear that such methods do not cure Parkinson's Disease, but they can be helpful for many sufferers, especially early on in its development. The drugs can certainly be a help, but they are not the whole answer. Some sufferers experience unwanted side-effects from these drugs— a reduction in mental ability in some cases, for example, and it can be a tricky business finding the right form of drug and the most helpful (or least unhelpful) level for each individual sufferer.

These considerations are of great importance in AD because in the mid-70s several research groups reported a reduction in a chemical associated with a particular neurotransmitter system in the brains of AD patients who had died. This system has also been associated with memory and learning, one of the central deficits in AD, so this finding naturally attracted great interest, especially when it was shown that there was a strong link between the chemical deficiency and the person's level of memory impairment before death. More recently, it has been clearly shown from studies where a tiny piece of brain has been removed whilst the person is alive (a brain biopsy) that this chemical deficiency does reflect a real change in the functioning of this system, and is not an artificial finding due perhaps to the person's death or final illness. The neurotransmitter in question is called acetylcholine, and the system is often referred to as the cholinergic system. Of even greater interest is the fact that a particular loss of brain cells, together with the presence of neurofibrillary tangles, has been identified in some of the deeper areas of the brain which form an essential part of the acetylcholine system. The evidence that this cholinergic pathway is of major importance in AD seems overwhelming.

Various researchers set about examining the therapeutic implications of these findings. Unfortunately, we are not simply dealing here with a chemical imbalance which can be rectified by feeding in appropriate amounts of the missing substance. It is a complex system that has broken down, and a great deal depends on where exactly in the system the problem lies. Early efforts focused on a substance that could under normal circumstances be used by the brain's cholinergic system. The hope was that it would reach the brain without undue side-effects, and that once there the cholinergic system would be able to use it to make acetylcholine, which would in turn help to increase brain function. One such substance was choline, a naturally occurring substance (found in some fish, for example) which is used in the manufacture of acetylcholine by the cholinergic brain cells. Unfortunately, it proved unpleasant to take regularly, often giving the patient a fishy smell and sometimes even a stomach upset. Its use did give a chance to resurrect the old wives' tale that eating fish is good for the brain!

Other substances that would be turned into choline by the body were then tried. Lecithin, another naturally occurring substance found in certain foodstuffs, was one. As with choline, the first results were generally disappointing. However, a study carried out at London's Institute of Psychiatry using high doses of lecithin did show some effects on the patients' abilities, at least in the short term. In examining why some patients seemed to show a better response than others, the research team noted that there could be a critical range of choline levels in the person's blood outside which the lecithin was ineffective, so that it was important to get the dose right for each patient. Studies of lecithin are continuing on this basis. Lecithin can literally be hard to swallow—the dosages used and the purity required are way beyond that found in packs of lecithin tablets in health food shops. In order to make it more palatable, the same team has experimented with using it as a substitute for fat in the making of appetising biscuits and cakes—a novel way to take your medicine!

A more sophisticated approach to the problem is to give a drug which will prevent the breakdown of acetylcholine. There normally exists a finely balanced system for both the production and the breaking down of acetylcholine so that the right amount is in the right place at the right time. If the production system is faulty, perhaps preventing it being broken down so quickly will allow more effective levels of acetylcholine to accumulate. There is a fair amount of evidence that one particular drug which acts in this way—called physostigmine—does indeed improve function in some AD sufferers. The big drawback with this drug is that it cannot be given on a regular basis.

In 1986 a report appeared from Summers and colleagues in the USA of the trial of a similar drug which had been used on a long-term basis with AD sufferers. The drug in question is called tetrahydroaminoacridine which, not surprisingly, is usually shortened to THA! The results of this trial were encouraging and in some cases dramatic: one sufferer went back to part-time work, another started to play golf again, for example. The researchers attributed their good results to ensuring as far as possible that everyone who took it had AD alone and no other complicating condition. They also monitored the dosage carefully, giving neither too much or too little, to achieve the best response.

In this study, as well as taking THA to stop acetylcholine being broken down, patients were also taking lecithin tablets to stimulate its production in the first place. As always, the drug is not without side-effects. Nausea is especially common, and further medication is sometimes required to keep it in check. THA is a well established drug, and has been used in anaesthetics for many years, but it has not been used on a long-term basis before. It is becoming clear that one of its side-effects in the longer term is on the functioning of the liver, and this problem will need to be resolved before wider-ranging trials of THA's usefulness can be carried through. Early studies of THA in the United Kingdom, again at the Institute of Psychiatry in London, attracted media attention when a distinguished scientist, a Nobel Prize winner in fact, revealed that he had AD but had benefited from taking THA. It had enabled him to start work on inventions again and resume some scientific work. However, we must await the results of carefully controlled evaluations of THA (see 'Drug trials' below) before assuming that THA is the 'miracle drug' everyone would like it to be.

Other approaches are of course being actively explored. Could the cholinergic system be 'persuaded' to operate more efficiently with the decreased amount of acetylcholine available? Or could the amount of acetylcholine available be boosted in some other way? One suggestion has been to implant in the person's brain a drug to encourage acetylcholine production, which is then slowly released over the course of time, avoiding the difficulty of crossing the blood-brain barrier. Another possibility that sounds at first even more like science fiction, but is not far off in fact, is the use of brain transplants—not the whole brain, it must be said, but rather the grafting of a small piece of live tissue of a type known to produce the relevant neurotransmitter onto a part of the brain where it can stimulate further transmitter production. In Parkinson's Disease, for example, it has proved possible to transplant into the brain from elsewhere in the person's body part of a gland which produces one of the chemicals which the sufferer's brain lacks. The line of research into AD being developed in Sweden and elsewhere is to remove the relevant brain cells from a foetus and implant them in the acetylcholine system. Experiments in animals suggest this could be a very useful approach. The foetal brain cells are still capable of growth and development, and this new growth can actually stimulate the acetylcholine system to operate more effectively.

It almost goes without saying that a major objection to this approach will be on ethical grounds. The use of brain cells from a foetus is bound to raise intense emotions. When several such operations were carried out in Birmingham on Parkinson's sufferers in 1988, there were strong reactions. To some it will seem a desecration of an unborn life, a compounding of the 'murder' of abortion. To others it will seem a sensible use of what would otherwise be destroyed, a way in which some good can come of a life that was not to be. Needless to say, the closer the link with abortion, the more contentious the procedure will be. Even if some way is found of growing the right cells, and so resolving the potential problem of the supply

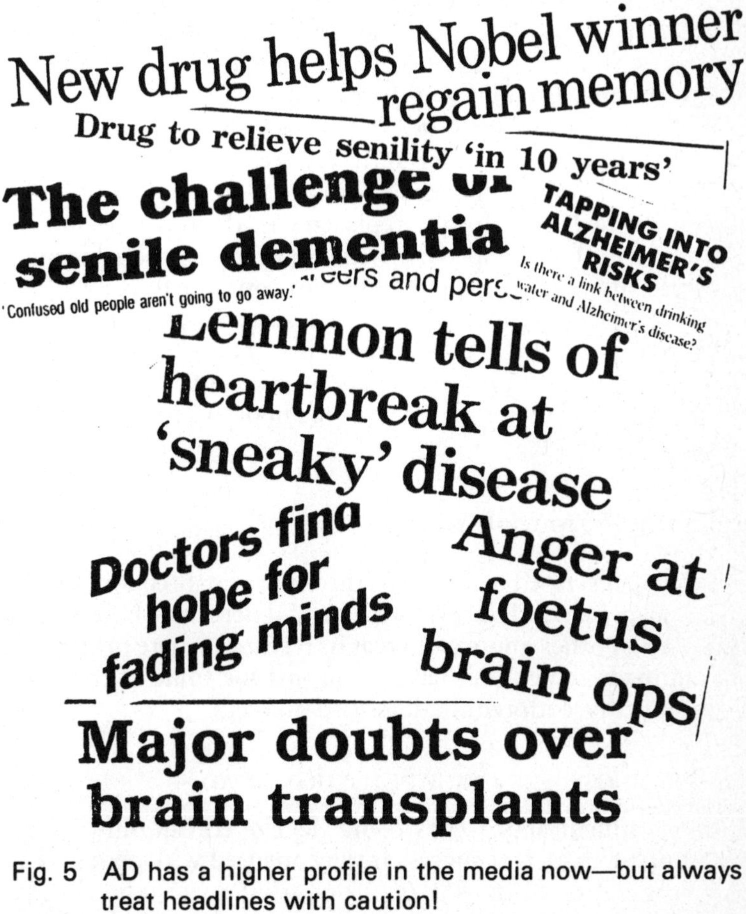

New drug helps Nobel winner regain memory

Drug to relieve senility 'in 10 years'

The challenge of senile dementia

TAPPING INTO ALZHEIMER'S RISKS

Is there a link between drinking water and Alzheimer's disease?

'Confused old people aren't going to go away.'

...eers and pers...

Lemmon tells of heartbreak at 'sneaky' disease

Doctors find hope for fading minds

Anger at foetus brain ops

Major doubts over brain transplants

Fig. 5   AD has a higher profile in the media now—but always treat headlines with caution!

of foetuses, the procedure will inevitably be costly, involving delicate brain surgery. Could it ever be available for the thousands of sufferers who might benefit?

All these developments are going to be accompanied by debates about ethics, resources, the value of human life, the risks of surgery against the potential benefits, and most importantly for relatives of AD sufferers, the value we as a society should place on treating this debilitating condition.

The whole debate will have to take place in the context of our knowledge that there are in any case severe limitations to this whole approach as far as the treatment of AD is concerned. Firstly, it is now well established that a number of other neurotransmitter systems are also affected in addition to acetylcholine; it could well be necessary to stimulate several systems simultaneously for an all-round improvement to occur. Interestingly, older sufferers are more likely to have only acetylcholine deficits, so they have the most hope of being helped by simple replacement therapy. Secondly, experience of this approach with sufferers from Parkinson's Disease suggests that the disease will continue to progress as times goes on, eventually reaching a stage where replacement therapy is no longer helpful. This means those already severely impaired are least likely to respond to this form of treatment. It is therefore even more important to identify AD in its early stages.

Clearing the way forward

We have described in detail the three prime contendors for the next leap forward in AD research. There are, however, a number of other important areas of research where progress is being made which will have a spin-off for some of the more newsworthy endeavours described above.

1   DIAGNOSIS AND EARLY DETECTION OF AD

The treatment approaches being developed can only have a reasonable chance of success if they are used with people who actually suffer from AD (and not from some other similar condition), and if the treatment begins early enough. Efforts are being made to develop agreed rules for the diagnosis of AD so that there can be international confidence that patients included in a treatment study would be similarly diagnosed elsewhere. In the UK, the Medical Research Council has laid down the type of information that must be recorded for each patient in a research trial to allow an acceptable diagnosis of AD to be made and, internationally, diagnostic criteria are being reviewed and refined in the light of present knowledge.

As specific treatments for AD begin to be developed, it becomes more important to distinguish AD from other forms of dementia. AD and multi-infarct dementia often occur together, making this a particularly difficult distinction. The advent of CT scans has helped a little, showing some of the areas of brain damaged by infarcts in certain cases of MID. In many instances the infarcted areas are too small to be visible on these scans, but the hope is that more sophisticated (and expensive) forms of scanning will have a higher definition. The MRI scan may be helpful in this context. It is currently being used experimentally in a very few centres in the UK. Table 3 details the various techniques that are becoming available for visualising or 'imaging' the brain, together with their pros and cons.

Table 3: Brain imaging techniques in AD

EEG (Electroencephalograph)	Records tiny amounts of electrical activity from scalp; electrodes attached to scalp at different points are able to show differences in activity of different brain regions. Response to light and sound can be of interest. Most useful in indicating any specific areas of damage, especially where this might lead to the person having fits. Having wires attached may feel frightening to patient; the gel used to make good contact between electrode and scalp is messy and hard to remove.
CT Scan (Computerized Tomography—also CAT Scan where A = Axial	X-ray technique, which builds up an image of the brain at various levels, as if a slice were taken across the brain. Shows shrinkage of brain, enlargement of central, fluid-filled

cavities. Shows some areas of damage if large enough, caused by stroke, tumour, etc. Involves patient lying still with head inside machine for a few minutes—less than other techniques. Some overlap between normal and AD brains in CT Scan appearance.

MRI Scan
(Magnetic Resonance Imaging—also NMR scan)

Uses strong magnetic fields; uses no radiation, so can be repeated frequently very safely; gives a 3-D image; various techniques allow different sorts of brain matter to be distinguished; shows well damage from infarcts, changes to blood vessels, etc. Patient still has to be in confined space for some time. Much finer quality than CT scan.

PET Scan
(Positron Emission Tomography)

Detects radiation given out by radioactive chemicals injected into the patient. The 'picture' produced is like a map showing where the chemical is situated in different parts of the brain. By using different chemicals it is possible to look at different processes. For instance, AD patients have been shown to take up less glucose (a source of brain energy) than normal. Soon it may be possible to map out neurotransmitter systems using this technique, which has tremendous potential. On the negative side, it is complex, expensive, needs a cooperative patient, and is likely to be mainly used in research studies. Available in a very few centres.

SPET Scan (Single Photon Emission Tomography)	A simpler procedure than PET, although related to it. Uses chemicals which decay less rapidly, and has been used to show blood flow in different parts of the brain—potentially a useful indication of brain function, and may assist in distinguishing different types of dementia. More likely to be used clinically in AD than PET scans, but still a fairly new procedure.

Early detection involves identifying which of the various indications of AD become apparent first in the course of the disorder. Are there particular changes in memory, decision making, reasoning or personality? Or are there some physical changes that can be identified early on, perhaps through one of the sophisticated scanning procedures being developed? A number of psychological tests of memory, learning, reasoning and so on are being applied in the quest for early detection (although as yet there are few efforts to explore the possibility of subtle personality changes that some carers report as the first sign). Ideally, these would need to be given to a large number of people in the age group most at risk, and perhaps repeated at regular intervals, so that in time people developing AD could be identified; and by looking back at their performance at different points in time indications of early signs of change might be spotted. This is a logical approach to the problem, but it would take longer than the normal 3-year period beloved of most research funding bodies, and is dependent on a good choice being made at the outset of the sorts of tests that are most likely to be sensitive to early AD-related change. People's memory and thinking abilities do fluctuate for all manner of reasons—a cold, being under the weather or under stress, or being on medication for some physical complaint, for example. If these produced the same sort of changes as AD in its earliest stages it would only be possible to detect the disease once its effects were sizeable enough to be outside the range of other everyday causes. And it is *change* above all that must be identified because people's abilities start at such different levels. So either the person has to be assessed at least twice, or change has to be assumed by comparing some ability that is known not to be affected much at all by early AD (such as reading words correctly) with those such as memory and learning that are affected at an early stage. Some of the psychological tests currently being used are in the form of 'video games' which are designed to assess the person's abilities in as enjoyable a way as possible. The computer systems used are able to measure accurately how long it takes the person to answer, as well as whether the answer given is correct or not. It may be that changes in the person's speed of decision-making occur before the person's ability shows a decline. Many of the systems being developed make use of touch-sensitive screens. The fact that the person touches the appropriate answer on the screen itself means that there is no need to learn how to use even a simplified keyboard.

One difficulty associated with all these assessments is how to distinguish the early signs of AD from what might be seen in normal people of the same age group. A number of normal older people show the reduction in brain size that has been associated with AD sufferers, for example, on the CT scan. Perhaps some of the more sophisticated scanning procedures will get around this problem. One test that is attracting interest is derived from the EEG 'brain-wave' test, where recordings are made of electrical activity at various points on the patient's head. The EEG recording does not itself pick up early AD in a reliable way, but there have been suggestions that the responsiveness of certain of the person's brain waves when a noise or a visual image is presented to the patient may be a sensitive indication of AD. In this context, it is not good enough for the test simply to give differences between groups of well-established AD sufferers and normal people. It has to be sensitive to early AD (which may only be confirmed as the disorder progresses) and it must not identify more than a tiny percentage of normal people or people with other disorders as being AD sufferers. While it is important to detect AD early, it is also important not to label people as having AD or some other form of dementia incorrectly.

2 ASSESSING CHANGE

In order to evaluate the effects of various treatments as they are developed, we need ways of measuring the amount of disability and impairment caused by the dementia. If we have a treatment to help people lose weight, its effects are measured in kilograms on the scales; a treatment to increase height is measured in feet and inches (or centimetres) on a tape-measure. Measuring dementia is not so straightforward. Of course, if there were a complete cure it would be only too obvious if a change had occurred. But in dealing with a situation where the aim may in the first instance be to slow down the rate of deterioration, accurate and sensitive systems of measurement are crucial. But measurement of what? Memory, learning, reasoning, verbal skills and such like can be measured by using various psychological tests, including the computerised tests mentioned above.

It is important to set the difficulty of the test at the right level: If it it is far too difficult the person will probably not want to be re-tested later; and if the person scores zero at his first attempt the test clearly cannot hope to be sensitive to any change in the person's abilities. Similarly, if the test is too easy and the person scores close to the maximum, there is no scope for the test to show any improvement. When we measure someone with a tape measure, we get almost exactly the same height, irrespective of how many times the person has been measured before. With psychological tests, it is quite common for people to improve with each repetition of the test. The person relaxes and becomes more practised at it. Even people with severe memory problems may show some improvement with practice. Efforts are now being made to produce several versions of each test to minimise the improvements that may be the result of practice alone and not the treatment. Many of the tests were originally devised to aid diagnosis and so they tended to concentrate on the tasks dementing people would perform badly. This has led to a tremendous need to develop further psychological tests which cover a wider range of abilities, and which allow people with AD to show both upward and downward change. Again, many of these tests are computerised. Experience with these tests shows that if they are set at the right level, and are well designed so that the person can see clearly what he or she is meant to do, testing is actually enjoyed by the majority of AD patients. A well-designed test can avoid the obvious confrontation with failing abilities which is uncomfortable and distressing for sufferer and tester alike.

Of course, it is not only the sufferer's memory and her intellectual problems that are of concern. Treatment should also be aimed at increasing the person's ability to look after herself, and at reducing such dementia-related problems as wandering, incontinence and even aggression. Some self-help skills—dressing, feeding, making a cup of tea—can be 'tested' of course by asking the person to carry out the task in question, but generally these aspects have been measured by asking someone who knows the person well—a carer or a nurse in hospital, for example—to rate each aspect of the person's abilities on some form of scale. This may not prove as easy as it looks. The scale may ask you to rate how the sufferer has been over the last seven days; but there may have been big differences from day to day. Sometimes your person doesn't seem to fit any of the categories given on the scale. Sometimes you're left wondering whether the sufferer might manage, say, to dress more independently if you allowed more time—but you can't, of course, because the day-centre transport might come early . . . Or the scale may ask how aggressive the person is. One carer may write 'not at all' because the sufferer never actually hits them; another may rate the same sort of behaviour as 'aggressive all the time' because the sufferer looks at the carer threateningly.

Sometimes then these scales seem to lack the precision they need, and research is going on at present to refine them and remove some of the guesswork which reduces their value as methods of scientific appraisal.

3   DRUG TRIALS

In evaluating any new treatment it is important to have a comparison group of untreated patients to show what changes may be due to practice rather than treatment. A successful treatment for AD might *slow down* the decline in abilities. This change could only be evident in comparison with a group of untreated patients. In drug trials it is customary for a placebo

—a dummy tablet without active ingredients—to be given to patients in the comparison group. In medicine, it has been demonstrated again and again that improvements can be obtained for reasons quite unconnected with the actual treatment being tested. The extra attention, regular visits by the doctor, regular blood tests, an air of hopefulness and expectancy—all these may be amongst the factors that can lead to the 'placebo' effect that must be allowed for in any drug trial. Of course, the patient (and carer) must not know it is a placebo or it will not be a fair test. Usually the doctor or nurse giving out the drug will not know either, so there is no danger of them communicating the true nature of the substance inadvertently, or of being biased by their expectations of its effect. This makes the trial 'double-blind': both doctor and patient are unaware of whether the drug is the real thing or a placebo. This may sound like a complicated procedure, but if we are to make progress with drug-treatments for AD, it is one that will have to be followed again and again so that only treatments with proven effectiveness are offered to sufferers and their carers. In some countries, false hopes have been raised in the past by extravagant claims for drugs that had not been rigorously tested. This does no one (except perhaps the pharmaceutical companies concerned) any good and, if anything, it hinders the search for effective methods of treatment.

4 FINDING OUT MORE ABOUT AD

Away from the high-tech world of electron microscopes, genetic markers and brain cell biochemistry, there are still a number of more mundane—but very important—questions to which research efforts are now being applied. Even the basic question of how often AD occurs needs to be asked again. The studies we rely on at present for this information were carried out 20 years ago, since when there have been great changes in the number of people over the age of 80, as well as developments in diagnostic techniques. These figures were for a representative sample of the over-65s, but we have very little information regarding how often AD occurs in middle-aged and younger people. On the assumption that aluminium may play a part in the development of AD, research is now looking at the possible correlation between the frequency of AD in different regions and the relevant minerals present in the water supplies and the environment.

To answer the question 'how widely spread is AD?' satisfactorily is an enormous undertaking. A large, representative sample of people in the age group in question must be interviewed, care being taken to include both those living in hospitals and homes for the elderly and those living at home or with relatives. Not everyone will want to be interviewed; the electoral roll or the general practitioners' lists may be out-of-date or inaccurate. Many different factors must be taken into account, and our present need is not just to identify how many people have some form of dementia, but to define the nature of the disorder more precisely. To identify true regional differences will then take some very careful research, involving the assessment of literally thousands of people. Already there have been suggestions that dementia is more common in older people in New York than in London, but the explanation for this is as yet unclear.

Although we know enough about AD to say that certain problems are more likely to occur early on and others at a later stage, and to give figures for the average life expectancy for a given age group, many unanswered questions still remain. Researchers are now beginning to follow through AD sufferers systematically, from the point of detection onwards, making use of some of the new physical and psychological measurement approaches described above. Are abilities always lost in a certain order or are there perhaps different patterns of change in different groups of patients? One theory is that there are two main types of AD sufferers. In the first group, the disorder begins at a younger age, progresses more rapidly, and affects speech, verbal abilities and practical skills (drawing, writing and dressing, for example) at an early stage, as well as memory, or course. The second group tends to be older when the disorder starts. This group has principally memory-related problems, and they decline at a slower rate. The suggestion is that this ties in with the findings of brain chemistry, the first group having deficits in a number of neurotransmitters, the second group mainly lacking acetylcholine. If this distinction is valid, it can only be at best a rough and ready guide because cases that do not fit these groups are legion! A more detailed grouping of cases may be needed, including one which shows more of the problems associated with damage to the frontal region of the brain—loss of previous social controls and inhibitions, gross change in personality, 'silliness', etc. There is a suggestion now that a sub-type exists where there are plaques but no tangles in the brain. It would certainly aid our ability to understand the likely course of an individual's disorder if some fairly reliable categories could be identified.

How to get the best from the AD sufferer

Another area where there has been a steady and developing research interest is in finding ways of bringing the performance of the AD sufferer to its optimum level. This interest really began in institutions for elderly people where it was clear that many residents—including some with dementia—were capable of doing more for themselves. The theory initially was that the residents were under-stimulated because of the dull, featureless environment, or because they were withdrawn, or because of poor eye-sight and hearing. This was thought to increase the level of confusion and was regarded as a possible explantion for increased restlessness at night, when there was even less to stimulate the senses and less people around with whom to interact. Efforts to increase activity and stimulation generally had some encouraging, but by no means dramatic, results. Often staff were surprised at how much patients could achieve with some help and encouragement, and many staff found increased pleasure and fulfilment in being more actively involved.

Stimulation and activity were taken further in Reality Orientation (RO) programmes, which originated in the USA as long ago as 1958. These programmes had two main components: small group sessions, where the group would re-learn relevant information and carry out activities together; and a general approach where staff would endeavour at all times to help patients be aware of where they were and what was happening to them. Both inside and outside these group sessions, staff would make use of memory aids—calendars, clocks, diaries, information boards, etc. RO was introduced into the UK in the mid 1970s, since when a number of evaluations of its effects have been published in various psychological and medical journals. It does seem to have had measurable effects on the persons' awareness of the information which they are taught—indicating that many AD sufferers do have some learning ability. Some sufferers have been successfully taught to find their way around a ward or a home with very simple training, using signs as memory aids. The main effects of RO are usually found in those areas actually taught; it is not often reported to have more general effects. But, once again, staff are often surprised and pleased by the response of AD patients to this type of approach.

A related approach that has attracted some interest during the 1980s is Reminiscence Therapy. This involves using pictures and other reminders of the past to stimulate discussion with the dementia sufferer, either on a one-to-one basis, or again in a small group session. In the UK a variety of reminiscence aids are available, covering the present century, everyday life and the historical events that have impinged on people's lives—wars, the Depression, royalty, etc. Pictures, mementoes, music and archive sound recordings (of Winston Churchill or King Edward VIII's abdication speech, for example) have been used. The emphasis is on helping the person recall and recount his or her own personal experiences —not have a group history lesson! Reminiscence does seem to be a good way of getting communication going, and of putting the AD sufferer for once in a superior position—of having been there and experienced things for himself. Both RO and Reminiscence also increase staff members' knowledge of individual patients, which is very important if care is to be given in a personalised fashion. There is an increasing use of 'This is your Life' books—personal scrap-books, with pictures and words describing the person's life and experiences. This can be a powerful way of helping staff get to know a new patient quickly, providing prompts for the patient to tell the staff about what he or she has done in life; what has been of value; the people and places that have been important.

It is generally accepted that while RO and Reminiscence are useful in some respects, both have their limitations. In reminiscence work, it is important to bear in mind that for some looking back will be a painful process. There may be some very unhappy memories, and it is helpful to find out in advance what may be difficult for each patient so he or she is not suddenly exposed to great distress in front of a group of people. Another concern has been that it will encourage patients to live in the past, but there is no evidence that this is the case. RO has been thought to encourage too many interactions where the AD sufferer is put right by the staff-member (although in fact this is not an essential feature of RO). In the USA a further approach, Validation Therapy, has been used, which aims at understanding what the sufferer is trying to express rather than trying to correct her error if the words do not make immediate sense. Perhaps some feeling or emotion can be heard or felt amongst the words and actions that at first seem rambling and meaningless; by tuning into these feelings, real communication can occur; the sufferer can at least have the experience of someone trying to understand, trying to empathise, rather than dismissing their efforts at expression as meaningless rubbish. Currently, nursing staff at London's Maudsley Hospital are attempting to practise Validation Therapy with a small group of AD sufferers, to explore its feasibility and its usefulness.

RO's demonstration that AD sufferers have some learning ability has led to an emphasis in research on using learning-based re-training programmes with AD sufferers. The current approach is to identify targets of relevance for each individual sufferer, and to build up the person's performance in small steps, keeping the memory load to a minimum by using memory aids. In some cases, systematic encouragement of the person by providing prompts and reminders is sufficient to improve the sufferer's level of function. The important thing is to use the minimum amount of help to get the person started. For example, residents in a nursing home became more independent in washing themselves when given encourage-ment and verbal reminders at each stage of the task. With groups of patients other than those suffering from AD, the use of tangible rewards has often been helpful. A smile or a word of approval usually seems to be reward enough for AD sufferers (as it is for most of us!), although it is important to link it with the task just achieved. Given the huge learning deficit in AD, and its progressive nature, dramatic changes are not going to be possible with learning (or any other) methods. However, by selecting the most important areas, those that will make most difference to sufferer and carer alike, worthwhile changes can occur. In the USA studies have shown how family members can be successfully taught to use learning-based methods with dementia-sufferers, and this is an area where further research would be helpful.

Finally, mention must be made of the effects of the environment on the AD sufferer. There is no doubt that patients do react differently to different environments, and there has been some interest in designing environments that minimise the person's disabilities by use of signs and notices; making different areas of the home look quite different from each other; making toilets accessible and easy to find; arranging chairs so there is a relaxed, comfortable atmosphere and so on. Probably the most important factor is the attitude of the people around the sufferer. By being patronising or over-powering or by being over-ready to do things for the sufferer, remaining abilities can be further impaired and problems magnified. Research on how to help staff develop the most helpful approach to AD sufferers is at an early stage, but it is sorely needed, both to improve the quality of life of AD sufferers, and for the peace of mind of their relatives.

Research on carers—their problems and their needs

In the previous section research focused largely on AD sufferers in homes and hospitals. The last few years has seen a welcome shift of attention towards the less visible needs and problems of the majority of sufferers who are being supported 'in the community'. Research studies have examined what sort of problems in the AD sufferer make life most difficult and stressful for the carer (sleep disturbance, restlessness, constant demands and faecal incontinence are usually near the top of the list). Other aspects of the caring situation have also been studied—the amount and type of help received; the health of the carer; attendance at a day-centre; whether carer and sufferer live together; the nature of their relationship (wife, husband, daughter, son, etc.) and its quality and their approach to coping with the problems they face. It has been discovered that the carer's distress does not necessarily go on increasing as the disorder progresses. Perhaps the carer develops better ways of coping, or some of the more difficult problems (wandering and aggression, for example) become less prominent as the person becomes increasingly disabled. It seems that the decision by the carer to allow the sufferer to go into a home or hospital is not simply a result of increasing distress—many carers carry on putting up with appalling levels of strain in order to keep the person at home.

These studies are beginning to lead to further research aimed at reducing carers' level of stress and many of these ideas have been incorporated in this book. In the next section we will discuss new developments in the care of AD sufferers which should also play a significant part in keeping distress to a minimum. Some studies have suggested that something like a half of all carers have a level of distress usually associated with psychiatric problems. Clearly ways must be found of preventing the carers' level of distress reaching this level even if the impact of AD on a family means it cannot ever be completely removed.

Services for the 1990s

It would be foolhardy to predict what services will actually become available in the next few years. Services are already distributed and organised on a very patchy basis in the UK, and debates are going on as to which services should be the responsibility of the health service, the social services, voluntary agencies and the private sector respectively. It is little wonder that many carers are not able to understand the complexities of a service system that defies rationality! The emphasis here is on highlighting some of the promising developments that will be of benefit to carers and sufferers if and when they are applied.

COMMUNITY SERVICES
The most encouraging developments are those which provide a service which is flexible, reliable and geared to the individual needs of carer and sufferer. 'Care manager' is a role we should hear more of. His or her job would be to develop a

package of care to meet the current needs of the situation, incorporating the carer's needs and, as far as possible, the sufferer's wishes. The co-ordinator's job would be to guide the carer through the maze of services and benefits, liaise between the various service agencies involved, and to monitor each element of the package to ensure that it is running smoothly. The carer would then deal primarily with this co-ordinator, rather than having to deal separately with perhaps half a dozen different agencies. The co-ordinator might work for a voluntary agency, the social services or one of the other agencies involved; all need to agree that the person is the key worker for this particular case. The care package will rarely remain static for long because the situation changes and develops so rapidly. The co-ordinator will need to review the package regularly with the carer and arrange additional help, or stop a service that is no longer needed. He requires skills in establishing what the needs of the carer are, and creativity in identifying what would be helpful in meeting these needs (see Table 4).

One way in which more flexible help can be provided is by greater use of local people to provide help consistently at the times when it is most needed (not when it fits into the work schedule). For example, a neighbour could regularly call in at 10 o'clock each evening to make sure that the sufferer who lives alone is safely bedded down for the night; or she could provide a meal at weekends, and sit with the sufferer whilst it is eaten (something the meals on wheels service cannot do!). The volunteer neighbour may be paid a small amount for this service so that she is not out of pocket. Such volunteers might also sit with the sufferer while the carer goes out, or spend time with the sufferer to relieve pressure on the carer.

Table 4—an example of a 'care package' for an AD sufferer

Need	Service	Agency
Carer needs help getting sufferer in and out of bath	Bath attendant, weekly	district nursing

Need	Service	Agency
Bath aids needed to make bathing safer	Community occupational therapist visits, assesses needs, orders aids required	social services
Carer needs relief three days a week so she can work part-time	Day centre, three times weekly	social services
Sufferer needs to be seen onto day-centre transport	Paid volunteer comes in three times weekly in the morning	voluntary agency
Carer needs relief two evenings a a week for social outings	Sitter stays with sufferer, helps get her to bed	voluntary agency
Carer welcomes help with cleaning house	Home help, weekly	social services
Carer needs advice and support in dealing with sufferer's difficult behaviour	Community Psychiatric Nurse visits, fortnightly	Health Authority
Sufferer's medication needs regular review (includes tranquillizers and sleeping tablets)	Out-patient appointment with Consultant Psychogeriatrician once every six weeks	Health Authority
Sufferer's mobility needs attention— has had falls before	Community Physiotherapist visits fortnightly	Health Authority

Need	Service	Agency
Carer needs relief for two-week summer holiday	Respite care in psychogeriatric unit	Health Authority
Carer needs relief for weekends away occasionally	Care-attendant 'lives in' over weekend	Private agency
Carer needs advice re. benefits and attendance allowance	Social worker to visit	Social services
Carer would like information regarding AD and to meet other carers	Put in touch with local ADS branch	Voluntary agency

Note: A number of different agencies and people may be involved—hence the need for a co-ordinator who understands the system, and who can ensure this complex procedure works as planned. Workers employed by the same authority may in practice have little contact with each other so there needs to be someone who oversees the whole situation, a person whom the carer may contact about any part of the whole package.

Both the care co-ordinator and the paid volunteer scheme have been established and evaluated very favourably in several areas of the UK. The Kent Community Care Scheme, for example, gives a co-ordinator a budget to spend on each person's care package, which can be spent on conventional services, home helps, or on paid volunteers, if required. Other schemes are based on paid care attendants coming into the person's home and providing the care there. Sometimes this has been facilitated by home-nursing and home-help services working together, and finding ways of crossing the boundary between domestic work and personal care that usually divides them; sometimes it is through the voluntary sector. In the UK 'Crossroads' was established to provide such home-care attendant service; often it can also be available through a private agency which may also provide help when it is needed most—at nights, for example. Only when 24-hour cover becomes possible will community care be really viable for the most severely disturbed sufferers. And even then you will need a home big enough to accommodate the teams of paid carers! However, the greater the choice of services, the more flexible the care-package becomes.

Day-centres specialising in dementia sufferers have been a great step forward—their special skills and knowledge can be a great asset. But there is a need also for more flexible forms of relief. A sitter coming into the person's home or a mini-day-centre in a paid carer's home, taking two or three people for the day can create a real social occasion! Similarly, respite care in homes or hospitals can be a real boon; but perhaps some of the increased confusion could be avoided if a paid-carer came to stay in the sufferer's home while the regular carer had a break. Regular, predictable periods of relief can be a real life-line for the carer, and some units purely for respite care are now being set up.

Efforts are being made by some of the specialist services to become more readily accessible. For instance, some diagnostic centres are establishing Memory Clinics to which anyone with a memory problem may be referred; some psychogeriatric services are setting up community teams (community dementia teams in some cases) with open referral policies, and a commitment to provide continuing support and help with an identified key worker.

RESIDENTIAL FACILITIES

The trend here is for homes which specialise in dementia to provide the extra care and have the sort of environment that can cope with wandering, restlessness, incontinence and all the other problems that make AD sufferers often unacceptable to other homes. 'Homely' is the word often used to describe the atmosphere and setting desired; this means being fairly small—although most are compromising this in the interests of economy. A home for 6 residents would be very expensive to staff! Some homes are being planned with several independent living units of eight to ten residents, sharing staff cover, meal preparation, laundry, etc. Homes are now being planned for some of the most severely disabled patients, who previously were cared for in hospital. The model of a hospice, where people retain a good quality of life despite being terminally ill, may be usefully applied. Staff will not see sufferers get better, but they may gain satisfaction from creating an atmosphere where each person is an individual; retaining their dignity despite disability; where families will feel welcome and able to share in the care if they so wish; where humanity is preserved in the face of a dehumanising disease. Such homes should be in the immediate locality of the family home so that family and friends may visit easily, and should have many links with the local community, not being 'shut away' as in the days (only now coming to an end) of the Victorian asylum. This 'domus' care will hopefully give carers an acceptable alternative when they can no longer keep the sufferer at home.

Contributing to the research effort

This is not an appeal for funds! However, the developments described in the previous pages would not have been possible without the participation of thousands of sufferers and their carers. One way you can aid progress in this field is to take part in research studies. Many researchers approach the Alzheimer's Society, nationally or locally, so they may have details of projects currently seeking subjects. Taking part in research projects has its drawbacks, of course. It may entail seemingly endless questionnaires, perhaps additional visits to the hospital for tests, keeping detailed records, and so on. But without people prepared to undertake these tasks the future is much less hopeful. If you have any doubts about the project, any worthwhile researcher will be happy to explain the project to you; projects should have been cleared by an ethical committee, which includes members of the public, to safeguard potential subjects.

Many advances have come from post-mortem studies of the brain. It is worth thinking well in advance whether you would be prepared for the sufferer's brain to be examined after death; discuss this with the doctor in charge of the case so that your wishes are known and you can be advised whether the brain could be used for research of this kind. Above all, avoid confusion at the point of death. By allowing an autopsy on a sufferer whose disorder has been well documented during his or her life-time, you will certainly be making a major contribution to the research effort, and hopefully bringing closer the time when AD can at least be controlled, if not cured.

Appendix

Useful organisations

1 *United Kingdom*
Alzheimer's Disease Society, England, Wales and N. Ireland: 158/160 Balham High Road, London SW12 9BN. Tel. 081-675 6557/8/9/0
Scotland: 1st Floor, 40 Shandwick Place, Edinburgh EH2 4RT. Tel. 031-225 1453
Many local branches and groups.

Other societies relating to specific conditions
Parkinson's Disease Society: 36 Portland Place, London W1N 3DG. Tel. 071-323 1174

The Huntington's Disease Association: 108 Battersea High Street, London SW11 3HP. Tel. 071-223 7000

Amnesia Association: 25 Prebend Gardens, Chiswick, London W4.
[Focuses on memory problems that are not part of an overall decline in abilities.]

Chest, Heart & Stroke Association: Tavistock House North, Tavistock Square, London WC1H 9JE. Tel. 071-387 3012
[Useful information and advice on problems related to strokes.]

Terence Higgins Trust: BM AIDS, London WC1N 3XX. Tel. 071-242 1010
[For people with AIDS and their carers.]

Other useful organisations
Age Concern has many local organisations throughout the UK. The local group will be able to give you details of local

services and facilities, advise on benefits and rights, etc. particularly where the sufferer is over retirement age. The appropriate national office will be able to put you in touch with the local group.

Age Concern England: 60 Pitcairn Road, Mitcham, Surrey CR4 3LL. Tel 081-640 5431
Age Concern Scotland: 54a Fountainbridge, Edinburgh EH3 9PT. Tel. 031-228 5656
Age Concern Wales: 1 Cathedral Road, Cardiff, CF1 9SD. Tel. 0222-371821/394659
Age Concern N. Ireland: 6 Lower Crescent, Belfast BT7 1NR. Tel. 0232-245729

The Carers National Association: 29 Chilworth Mews, London W1 3RG. Tel. 071-724 7776
[Incorporates Association of Carers and National Council for Carers and their Elderly Dependents. For all carers, irrespective of type of illness/disability involved. Many self-help groups throughout the UK. Also campaigns to ensure government and local authorities are aware, and act on, carers' needs.]

MIND—National Association for Mental Health: 22 Harley Street, London W1N 2ED. Tel. 071-637 0741.
[For all mental health problems; many local groups; campaigns to improve services for people with mental health problems—including those with dementia.]

Crossroads Care Attendant Scheme: 94 Coton Road, Rugby, Warwickshire CV21 4LN. Tel. 0788-73653
Scotland: 24 George Street, Glasgow G2 1EG. Tel. 041-226 2793
[Many local schemes providing care-attendants to help with care of disabled people at home: some schemes are able to help dementia sufferers. Very flexible in nature of help given—can be outside normal service hours!]

Counsel and Care for the Elderly: Twyman House, 16 Bonny Street, London NW1 9LR. Tel. 071-485 1566
[Information and advice about homes and services for the elderly, including financial implications. In London area,

maintains list of private and voluntary homes regularly visited, and will seek to identify suitable homes for a particular elderly person. Advice on topping-up grants, where benefits do not meet full cost of a private home.]

Carematch: 286 Camden Road, London N7 0BJ. Tel. 071-609 9966
[Computer service to find appropriate residential care for people with disabilities, including dementia.]

Grace Link: Upper Chambers, 7 Derby Street, Leek, Staffordshire, ST13 6HN. Tel. 0345-023300
[Can give details of private homes outside London.]

Disabled Living Foundation: 380-384 Harrow Road, London W9 2HU. Tel 071-289 6111
[Advice on adaptations, aids, etc. to reduce effects of disability. For example, aids for dealing with incontinence, specially adapted clothing, walking aids, etc.]

British Association for Counselling: 37A Sheep Street, Rugby, Warwickshire CV 21 3BX. Tel. 0788-78328/9
[Will put you in touch with a local counselling service.]

RELATE—The National Marriage Guidance Council: Herbert Gray college, Little Church Street, Rugby, Warwickshire CV21 3AP. Tel. 0788 73241/60811
[Many local branches offering a confidential counselling service on any matters—not restricted to marital problems!]

Citizen's Advice Bureau: National Association of CAB, 115-123 Pentonville Road, London N1 9LZ. Tel 071-833 2181
[Your local branch will be listed in the telephone directory or the national Association will give you the details. Will help you get started in tackling any problem—financial, legal, housing, etc.]

Samaritans: See local telephone directory.
[Whenever you need a sympathetic hearing, day or night, there is always someone available. Some branches now offer face-to-face sessions as well as the telephone help-line. Don't feel you have to wait till you're really desperate before calling.]

Holiday relief services
Holiday Care Service, 2 Old Bank Chambers, Station Road, Horley, Surrey RH6 9HW. Tel. 0293-774535
[Have details of a range of accommodation where nursing or personal help is available.]

Care Home Holidays Ltd., Wern Manor, Porthmadog, Gwynedd, Wales LL49 9SH. Tel. 0766-513322
[Offer details of over 30,000 holiday breaks for the elderly and infirm in need of care. *See also* Counsel and Care for the Elderly, Grace Link and Carematch.]

2 *Alzheimer Societies outside the United Kingdom:*
Each Society should be able to give details of organisations and literature specific to that country.

Australia: Alzheimer's Disease and Related Disorders Society of Australia, PO Box 470, Hawthorn, Victoria 3122, Australia. Tel. 3 818-0738

Canada: Alzheimer Society of Canada, 1320 Yonge Street, Suite 302, Toronto, Ontario M4T 1XL, Canada. Tel. 416 925-3552

France: France Alzheimer, 49, rue Mirabeau, 75016 Paris, France. Tel. 1 45 20 13 26

Ireland: The Alzheimer Society of Ireland, St John of God, Stillorgan, Co. Dublin, Ireland

New Zealand: Alzheimer's Disease and Related Disorders Society Inc., PO Box 31-102, Wellington, New Zealand

South Africa: Alzheimer's and Related Disorders Association, PO Box 81183, Parkhurst, Johannesburg 2193, South Africa

United States of America: Alzheimer's Disease and Related Disorders Association, 70E Lake Street, Suite 600, Chicago, Illinois 60601, USA

Selected reading
Many of the organisations listed above produce useful pamphlets, booklets and books. When contacting them ask for a list of publications so you can select those relevant to your own needs. Many of the national Alzheimer's Disease Societies produce their own literature, which will be helpful in identifying services and resources in that particular country.

1 Brief booklets on dementia for carers
Caring for the person with dementia—a guide for families and other carers (2nd ed. 1989) Chris Lay and Bob Woods. Alzheimer's Disease Society, London.
[Reduced cost to society members.]
Who cares? Information and support for the carers of confused people Health Education Authority Supplies Department, Hamilton House, Mabledon Place, London WC1H 9TX. Free of charge. Also available for carers from: PO Box 807, London SE99 6YE.
Coping with dementia: a handbook for carers (1987) Scottish Health Education Group, Woodburn House, Canaan Lane, Edinburgh EH10 4SG.
Coping with caring: a guide to identifying and supporting an elderly person with dementia (1981). Brian Lodge. MIND, 22 Harley Street, London, W1N 2ED.
24-Hour Approach to the Problems of Confusion in Elderly People (1982). Una Holden and others. Winslow Press, Telford Road, Bicester, Oxon. OX6 0TS.
[Less comprehensive than other booklets: focuses specifically on communication with the patient.]
'Grandpa doesn't know it's me'. Donna Guthrie. Human Sciences Press Inc., 72 Fifth Avenue, New York NY10011, USA.
[A delightfully illustrated story to help a child understand a little more about Alzheimer's.]

2 Longer books for carers
Dementia and Mental Illness in the Old (1986). Elaine Murphy. Macmillan, London.
[Covers other forms of mental illness in elderly people, including depression.]

Coping with Ageing Parents (1983). Chris Gilleard and Glenda Watt. MacDonald, but available from WR Chambers, 43-45 Annandale Street, Edinburgh EH7 4EZ.
[Includes sections on dementia, but also covers other potential problems with elderly parents.]

The 36-Hour Day: a family guide to caring for persons with Alzheimer's disease, related dementing illness and memory loss in later life (1981). Nancy L. Mace & Peter V. Rabins. USA Edition, the John Hopkins University Press, Baltimore. UK edition, *The 36-Hour Day: caring at home for confused elderly people* (1985). Adapted by Beverly Castleton, Christopher Cloke and Evelyn McEwen. Hodder & Stoughton, London, in association with Age Concern, England.
[A very detailed book that has been of great value to many carers. The British version puts details of services, etc. into a British context.]

Caring at Home (1988). Nancy Kohner, for the King's Fund Informal Caring Support Unit. National Extension College, 18 Brooklands Avenue, Cambridge CB2 2HN.
[A handbook for people looking after someone at home— young or old, handicapped or disabled, ill or frail. Readable and well designed book, although aimed at all carers irrespective of the condition they are dealing with.]

Care for the elderly: a citizen's advice guide (1987). J. Willingham. Macdonald Optima, London.
[Covers benefits, services, etc. available for elderly people.]

3   Books on finding respite care and/or finding a suitable home

Taking a Break: a guide for people caring at home (1987). King's Fund Informal Caring Programme. Free to carers from: Taking a Break, Newcastle-upon-Tyne X, NE85 2AQ.

Care Guides. Produced and published by Laing & Buisson. Ruskin Book Services Ltd., Unit 306, Hartlebury Trading Estate, Kidderminster, Worcestershire DY10 4JB. Tel. 0299 251505.
[Available in 11 regional editions; each has advice on the options available and a regional directory of homes, registration authorities, etc. Gives information on which homes will provide care for dementia sufferers.]

Croner's 'Care Homes Guides'. Croner Publications, Croner House, 173 Kingston Road, New Malden, Surrey. Tel. 01-942 8966. Two vols. North and South England (not rest of UK).
[A directory of residential and nursing homes etc. Pricey, so worth asking your local public library to obtain a copy for you.]
What to look for in a private or voluntary home (1986). Counsel & Care for the Elderly—address above. Send an SAE for a copy.
At Home in a Home (1988). Pat Young. Age Concern England (address above).
[A practical guide to residential homes and the alternatives, and what to look for when choosing a home.]

4   Legal and Financial Matters
The Law and Vulnerable Elderly People (1986). Age Concern England (address above).
[A useful guide to the current legal framework and its limitations.]
Your Rights. Annually from Age Concern England (address above).
[An invaluable guide to money benefits for retired people.]
Disability Rights Handbook. Annually from Disability Alliance, 25 Denmark Street, London WC2H 8NJ.
[Appropriate where the sufferer or carer is under retirement age.]
Elderly people—rights and opportunities (1986). Jill Manthorpe. Longman, Harlow.
DHSS booklets and leaflets on benefits are obtained from your local DHSS office or by post from: DHSS Leaflets Unit, PO Box 21, Stanmore, Middlesex HA7 1AY. Advice is also available on 'Freeline Social Security', 0800 666 555, during office hours; calls are free of charge.

For free information about dealing with the estates of people who suffer from mental disorders, including Enduring Powers of Attorney, apply to: the Court of Protection, 24 Kingsway, London WC2B 6HD.

5   *For a deeper look...*
The man who mistook his wife for a hat (1985). Oliver Sacks.
   Picador, Pan Books Ltd., London.
[A neurologist's case-histories raise many interesting questions about the nature of the mind in a person whose brain is damaged.]
Memory: a user's guide (1982). Alan Baddeley. Penguin, Harmondsworth.
[For those wanting to understand more of how memory works—and breaks down—this is a readable account by one of Britain's leading experts on memory.]
Understanding Senile Dementia (1987). A. F. Jorm. Croom Helm, London.
Understanding Dementia (1988). A. Jacques. Churchill Livingstone, Edinburgh.
[Two readable books, giving a good, clear background to dementia, which would be of use to an interested lay-person.]
Another Name for Madness (1985). Marion Roach. Houghton Mifflin Company, 2 Park Street, Boston, Massachusetts 02108, USA.
[A personal account of the experience of Marion Roach and her sister in caring for their mother, an Alzheimer sufferer, at home for six years.]
Have the Men Had Enough? (1989). Margaret Forster. Chatto & Windus, London.
[An acclaimed novel about a family's struggle to care for a relative suffering from dementia.]

Index